Steve Borg

BorgDirect Marketing

D0730199

STEVE!

NOW YOU'VE GOT

THE POWERS

all
the
Best,

tony

"I've seen all ends of the spectrum of brand challenges in my years as a CMO, from making the centuries-old National Geographic Society relevant for Millennials to launching digital brands for Boomers. In every instance, knowing how and when to wield some of these magical brand powers, while not falling under the spell of others, is absolutely essential. In an increasingly noisy, post-digital world, businesses that are winning are winning on brand. *The Powers* is a fantastic exploration of the magic that goes into building the kind of enduring brand that will be part of generations to come."

—**Amy Maniatis**, CMO, Charlotte Russe

"Companies that strive to be and stay mighty must do so surrounded by a powerful brand. *The Powers* presents an excellent framework for building and tending this underpinning of mightiness."

—**Robert Sher**, Author, Mighty *Midsized Companies: How Leaders Overcome 7 Silent Growth Killers*, San Francisco, CA

"I have known Peter for over 20 years and have great respect for his keen skills and ability to assess and position a brand. Both Peter and his partner Tony Wessling have the experience that can be an asset to any organization. If you're interested in growing and strengthening a regional or global brand that will truly resonate with customers and employees alike, then *The Powers* is a perfect read."

—**Jim Hackbarth**, CEO, Assurex Global, Columbus, OH

"I received an advanced copy of *The Powers* manuscript in digital form, and settled in to read it on my iPad. Eventually I decided that it would be easier to take notes if I read it on my Macbook. Finally, I chose to print a copy so I could write, old school, all over the now-well-turned pages with a mug of tea close by. *The Powers* is a business book that has managed the impossible: It's also a page turner. You are going to like this book, and you are going to read it more than once. And then I suspect you are going to keep a copy close at hand, and reference it frequently."

—**Dennis Moseley-Williams**, Principal, DMW Strategic Consulting, Ottawa, Ontario, Canada

"The fact that brand is critical in building distinct value and differentiation from the velocity of noise created by new media types is self-evident. But how to accomplish this has been viewed as something more of an art form than a pragmatic series of tasks. No longer. Wessling and van Aartrijk take a lifecycle approach to brand building/maintaining that provides a road map for those in charge of strategy or tactics. Read this book and take responsibility for your brand."

—**Peter Weyant**, Technology Solutions Executive, Tampa, FL

"I've been observing with keen interest the work of Tony and Peter ever since they founded Chromium. Many of their unique observations and ideas have been published in the pages of our magazines over the years. They avoid the fluff often seen in branding books; instead, *The Powers* is a nice, clean, useful and enjoyable read. This gem is a genuine benefit for anyone looking to create a more relevant brand."

—**Mark Wells**, Chairman, Wells Media Group, San Diego, CA

"Savvy entrepreneurs know that building a strong brand is equally as important as developing a superior product. *The Powers* provides a valuable framework based on ten factors for success by which a leadership team can create relevance with their customers and investors now – while at the same time building tremendous brand value for the long run."

"Peter van Aartrijk and Tony Wessling are signals in the noise when it comes to building a brand. They are my gurus for creating high-level brand and culture strategy – and turning that into tangible results."

THE POWERS

Ten Factors for Building an
Exponentially More Powerful Brand

TONY WESSLING and
PETER VAN AARTRIJK

NEW YORK

LONDON • NASHVILLE • MELBOURNE • VANCOUVER

THE POWERS
Ten Factors for Building an Exponentially More Powerful Brand

© 2019 **TONY WESSLING and PETER VAN AARTRIJK**

Published in New York, New York, by Morgan James Publishing. Morgan James is a trademark of Morgan James, LLC. www.MorganJamesPublishing.com

The Morgan James Speakers Group can bring authors to your live event. For more information or to book an event visit The Morgan James Speakers Group at www.TheMorganJamesSpeakersGroup.com.

ISBN 978-1-68350-995-0 paperback
ISBN 978-1-68350-996-7 eBook
Library of Congress Control Number: 2018934772

Cover Design by:
Rachel Lopez
www.r2cdesign.com

Interior Design by:
Bonnie Bushman
The Whole Caboodle Graphic Design

In an effort to support local communities, raise awareness and funds, Morgan James Publishing donates a percentage of all book sales for the life of each book to Habitat for Humanity Peninsula and Greater Williamsburg.

Get involved today! Visit
www.MorganJamesBuilds.com

TABLE OF CONTENTS

FOREWORD

Twenty-five years ago while working in the communications department at Apple, I started hearing the term "branding" thrown around and the question frequently asked by product and marketing managers, "What is our value add?" It was the beginning of what would become an industry unto itself, one devoted to finding the intrinsic value associated with a company and its products. People, as part of the brand, had no part in the conversation.

Fast forward to 2018 when getting branding right is recognized as critical by everyone from senior leadership to recruiters. And people within the company are considered brand advocates. With these realizations has come big spending. In fact, as much as $595 billion was reported to be spent in 2016, with projections of around $740 billion by 2020, according to key findings from the *U.S. Brand Activation Marketing Forecast 2016* issued by the Association of National Advertisers. Companies are making this level of brand investment even when they can't predict the outcome of the spend (despite all the great analytical software and big data crunching tools out there) and knowing the investment may not be realized until after a major crisis (see the chapter *The Power of Eight*), or over an extended period of time (the issue addressed in the first chapter *The Power of Ten*).

Branding as an important function of a company's well-being isn't at issue. The debate now is how to build an iconic brand and much has been written on the topic including extensive dissections of those that have risen and fallen. However, while opinions and best practices abound and there's been a lot of iterative work on the subject, real breakthroughs have been few and far between. Until now.

The Powers is the first book I've found that shows leadership teams how to create a powerful legacy brand from the inside out by focusing on the ten key factors that every successful brand possesses. And at a time when brand pride is a requirement in recruiting and retaining top talent, companies cannot overlook the relationship between culture and brand that Chromium advocates (and this book explores in *The Power of Four*). I can't wait for the follow-up book that goes even deeper into that subject – hit those keys, guys!

Tony once paid me the largest compliment of my career. After a speech where I demonstrated how "Big Purpose" branding could give companies more to say and do, he came up to me and said "I wish I'd thought of that." This book gives me the opportunity to use these same words to return the compliment. He and Peter have created a brand-building process that shapes and solidifies a company's DNA in a positive and impactful way (as you'll find when you reach the chapter *The Power of One*).

May all *The Powers* be with you in all things branding.

—**Whitney Greer**, CEO, RebelMind
Communications and co-Author of *Wabi-sabi at Work*

INTRODUCTION

As we lurch toward the end of two decades of careers in what is loosely called the "marketing communications" industry, we've found that while we know a tremendous amount about how strong brands are built and maintained, there is still something inexplicable, something magical, about successful brands. They're just so good at what they do, and they always seem to be in tune with the Zeitgeist. Like any good story, the possibility for tragedy could also lurk just around the corner for these brands; the Apple or Facebook of today could quite possibly join such former war horses as Kodak, Pontiac, Yahoo!, Blackberry, AOL, Sony, and Lehman Brothers (just to name a few) in either the also-ran category or the glue factory of commercial history.

In the end, the story of a brand is a very human story of birth, life's achievements, and, eventually, death. Perhaps that's why we find brands so compelling.

We define "brand" as a network of experiences woven together to form a persistent, singular concept. It's like the delicate senses of a spider's web: Every intersection on the web is a memory—a sight, sound, smell, taste, touch, or feeling that is associated with a particular brand. When woven together, a touch on any part of that web is transmitted across the network, and the concept of the brand instantly pops out, like the spider that senses when a bug has been ensnared. When well managed, the brand can become the most important asset your company owns.

Furthermore, we categorize brands in one of two ways: "Quo Brands" and "Innovator Brands." Quo Brands are led by individuals who are resistant to change or simply don't understand that they need to change. They talk about the "good old days," decline to invest in brand and culture strategy, don't offer prospective employees a good reason to want to work there, see revenue slipping or become stagnant, and so on. It's malaise and milquetoast. These are firms who may be among the walking dead, but may not realize it yet.

Innovator Brands are the opposite: vibrant, growing, and exciting places to work because their authentic and shared core values guide employee behavior. They encourage risk-taking to learn new ways to develop and market things. They attract new customers. They have raving fans. They can command premium pricing. They're market leaders, or on their way to leading. We could go on about how we feel about Innovators, but we'll stop there.

Finally, a word about the title and structure of this book. Unlike mathematical Powers of Ten, the Powers that we ascribe to branding do not get more powerful in a linear progression. The Power of One is equally as potent as the Power of Seven. But taken together, they will make your brand significantly more powerful than it was before.

Master another Power, and you've got a hundred times the mojo. Find your brand afflicted by the negative consequences associated with the Power of Eight, and you'll see it greatly diminished. We start with ten and end with one, giving the whole thing a kind of countdown feel, and when you get to the Power of One, you'll see how the whole complex process really distills down into a single, unifying, and yes, *powerful* concept.

We're looking forward to seeing *The Powers* help your organization find its true strategic North Star—and along the way an exciting brand and a vibrant culture.

—**Tony Wessling** and **Peter van Aartrijk**
San Francisco, CA and Washington, DC

ACKNOWLEDGEMENTS

We'd like to thank those who were instrumental in the success of *The Powers*:

- Our clients who have trusted us to guide their most important business assets—brand and culture—for we have enjoyed the journey together.
- Our talented and creative Chromium colleagues and co-conspirators, including Fiona Berry Gray, Robert Fritze, Courtney Lewis, Chad Stose, John Novaria, Christina Kettler and Amy Skidmore, for providing excellent comments and insights, and Kate Oppenheimer for her contributions to the chapter *The Power of Four*.

- The late and great Maureen Wall Bentley for her wisdom about brand and, even more so, her courage in the face of impossible odds.
- Chelsey Davidson for research assistance and youthful exuberance; Sissi Haner for running a vacuum cleaner over what we had considered "perfect" punctuation and sentence structure; and Morgan James Publishing for getting the manuscript to the point where you have something beautiful to read over coffee.
- *Carrier Management* and *National Underwriter* magazines for providing us an occasional forum in which to speak our minds; "Peter's Takes" and some other material in this book are adapted from pieces that originally appeared in those publications.
- And Ellen Wallace van Aartrijk and Michele Monique Imfeld Wessling for supporting our efforts and putting up with our seemingly endless proclamations that we were almost finished with this book. We've realized that when it comes to branding, the book is always being written.

THE POWER OF TEN

Prepare for the long haul: It can take ten years or more to build a truly strong brand. And once established, brands should be refreshed approximately every decade to maintain relevance.

"A great brand is a story that never stops unfolding."
—**Tony Hsieh**, CEO of Zappos

The Internet Era of the 1990s seemed to give rise to instantly famous brands, as if they were mixed up in a lab somewhere and poured over the globe, like the Sherwin-Williams logo showing paint covering the world. As we write this in 2017, Google is ubiquitous, Amazon is dominant, and Uber is ascendant. Nearly everyone in first-world countries has had some form of contact with these brands. But the reality is that they didn't quite become household names overnight. Google was founded in 1998, Amazon in 1994. Even superstar "newcomer" Uber turned eight this year.

The point here is that brands aren't strong and valuable right out of the gate. They may attain some level of recognition fairly quickly, something accelerated by our mobile-connected world, and in this way a brand, even a young one, becomes one more buzzword flying around the media. There's no denying that this recognition certainly helps the marketing effort and builds early sales. But the fact of the matter is that very new companies don't really deserve to be designated as "true brands" until they've gained high levels of trust as well as high levels of awareness in the marketplace. This can often take up to ten years or more, and this is what we call the Power of Ten.

A true brand is much more than a name or a logo, and building a brand with real value takes years of diligence and hard work. Uber may have a great deal of recognition (or notoriety) at this point, for example, but it's still working on building trust with consumers, employees, regulators, and investors—and it hasn't exactly been a walk in the park. The Uber brand, therefore, is not entirely mature and so lacks enduring value at this point. Were the company to fail (which is not completely unimaginable), the most valuable components would be the technology, the data, the user base, and the network of drivers. The brand would be an afterthought, much like PetSmart acquiring Pets.com after the dot com bust of the early 2000s, where the URL and the customer base were valuable but the brand in and of itself lacked the Power of Ten.

It's important to keep this in mind as you seek to build a brand for your organization. You have to be in it for the long haul— sometimes even decades. Even if your organization has been around for some time, it's not unusual for there to have been very little active, intentional branding apart from maybe a name and a that-will-do-for-now logo. Thus, in such a case you're essentially starting at square one when it comes to acquiring the Power of Ten.

Brands don't just appear overnight. Our experience has been that branding is a process that can't be accelerated too quickly without running the whole thing off the road. It's methodical, starting with the development of a clear strategy authored by key stakeholders of the organization and owned by the entire organization. Your strategy will act as a steady guide for your brand and culture over many years, much like the Constitution of the United States of America has guided this country throughout its history. Sure, amendments are made and courts interpret things differently as times change, but the underlying principles remain the same. So it should be with a brand and culture strategy, which should be considered a durable asset that is altered only under remarkable circumstances, or with the passage of time to keep relevant.

Start with Key Stakeholders

It's essential that an organization's key stakeholders be brought together to author a proprietary brand and culture strategy that will underpin the Power of Ten. The strategic framework we help clients produce is a document that codifies nine key components: Mission, Vision, Values, Brand Persona, Brand Narrative, Brand Evidence, Positioning, Targeting, and at the center of it all, the Brand Essence, sometimes referred to as the brand's mantra, or its DNA.

The language in this framework should be concise. In fact, one of the hardest challenges we've found is editing the content of this framework down until it is in the most effective and efficient form possible. We actually insist that the strategy be a one-page document—not an easy feat. But this is a vitally important step, as all expressions of the brand will be driven by these words (with only occasional minor updates) for the next ten years. There should be little room for ambiguity.

Implementation of the strategy is done through consistent and repetitive tactical expressions—day after day, week after week, year after year—for about ten years. This focus on repetition doesn't mean the expressions should be boring; on the contrary, creativity is essential to customers developing emotional connections to the brand. But in the end, this creativity has to be driven by the strategy—not the other way around—because creativity is by its nature somewhat chaotic while brands require consistency in order to become powerful.

The strongest messaging is always developed with clear intent—to resonate with the deep human needs of your target audience—and needs to be repeated in your marketing over and over and over again, ad nauseam, until it elicits instant recall. You say "Volvo," I say "Safety." You say "Napa," I say "Wine." You say "Quaker," I say "Wholesome." This is the Power of Ten; these strong associations did not happen overnight, but were decades in the making.

Corporate identities, known generally as names, logos, and taglines, must be similarly developed to appeal to the target audience. They must clearly display the Brand Persona and be expressed with consistency and frequency to achieve salient awareness and leverage the Power of Ten.

We often play a little game when we give presentations to business groups to illustrate the importance of the Power of Ten in branding: We first show a slide with a brown background and the word "COFFEE" in white lettering. At that point, it's just coffee, the commodity, and nobody makes any clear brand associations. Change the background color to green, however, and suddenly it's not generic, lower-case coffee anymore—it's Starbucks Coffee. In fact, if you look at expressions of the Starbucks brand today, it has become so ubiquitous that it no longer needs to show either "Starbucks" or "Coffee" along with the green mermaid logo. The current use of the mark is devoid of any descriptive words, yet it is universally understood. That's a true brand, decades in the making: Starbucks was founded in 1971, and didn't even begin the journey to become a national brand until the mid-1980s.

Achieving the Power of Ten is clearly a tremendous investment in time and money, but the return on that investment can be equally tremendous. Various estimates of the value of the Coca-Cola brand—just the brand—peg it as currently worth around $78 billion. The hard assets of the company, meanwhile, reportedly carry a much smaller price tag of only about $10.5 billion. It's interesting how something you can't even touch could be worth so much cold, hard cash.

While your brand may never reach such heights, the literature is filled with statistics on how the value you build into your brand will return generous dividends in the form of lower customer acquisition costs, premium pricing advantage, the attraction and retention of better talent to your organization, stronger bargaining positions in mergers and acquisitions, higher share prices, and significantly higher valuations at exit.

Maintaining Relevance: The Ten-Year Rebrand Cycle

Look at the corporate identities for Pepsi and Coke. They are certain to be very familiar, as you likely are exposed to them nearly every day in some fashion or another. Same with Burger King and McDonald's. Apple and Microsoft, too. But for all their familiarity, the current iterations of these corporate identities are distinctly different than they were ten years ago, significantly different than they were twenty years ago, and in some cases, dramatically different than they were thirty years ago. Yet they remain unmistakably themselves while at the same time appearing somehow fresh and appealing (maybe not to you, but to their target market, certainly).

This is because they have harnessed the Power of Ten.

No brand is eternal. But brands can live the longest and fullest lives possible when a company's leadership leverages the Power of Ten and periodically revisits the brand strategy and brand identity. By periodically, we mean at least every ten years. By brand identity, we mean the strategy that underpins the broader image and message the brand is projecting, not just the corporate identity, which is comprised of the logo, colors, and tagline.

Times change, people change, society changes, and brands that don't change with them usually start to fall behind in sales and profits, as well. We call these stubborn head-in-the-sand holdouts "Quo Brands." Conversely, "Innovator Brands" are those willing to reinvent themselves. Perhaps an exception to this rule is for "olde timey" brands, such as Kiehl's, Mrs. Meyer's Clean Day, or Altoids. Whether they truly are old brands or were simply created to look as such, these brands are operating from a strategy that consciously calls for an unchanging, period-piece look.

Timing the Power of Ten

The exact timing of a Power of Ten rebrand can be determined by reading stakeholder sentiment within your company, as these are the people whose day-to-day work puts them in intimate contact with the changing needs or habits of customers. Of course, ongoing market research is also informative to this effort, and we can't overemphasize how important it is that leadership teams budget for this sort of activity. And, especially given the prevalence of real-time social media (or "SoMe," as we refer to it, because it's all *so* very much about *me!*), they must listen to, trust, and follow the guidance of the company's brand and marketing professionals in reading the trending sentiment of the target audience. Finding and addressing customer emotional needs that other brands are missing can provide a significant competitive advantage.

By focusing on these two points, experiential and analytical, you help ensure that the timing of any rebrand is based on significant internal or external events that have direct relevance to the way your brand figures in the lives of your customers. This rebrand, or refresh, is not to be confused with the more frequent changes in marketing copy, websites, or advertising that are required to hold the customer's ever-shorter attention span. That kind of activity tends to be based on more acute situations such as new product releases, fads, holidays, or competitor product releases, or it results from efforts to achieve a sales objective or some other metric milestone.

A rebrand is a strategic investment in the future that likely will not show the kind of immediate return that comes from a new marketing campaign, but provides ongoing relevance to a younger, upcoming audience. This makes the company more stable in the long term. When done correctly, it holds onto the legacy customer while at the same time onboarding a whole new generation.

Significant external brand events that portend wholesale cultural or socioeconomic shifts (like the recent Great Recession of 2008, the Civil Rights Movement, and the Internet Era, to name a few) represent such opportunities for newfound relevance. In fact, brands that don't reexamine their strategies during such disruptions do so at their own peril, because even if the immediate effect on relevance is negligible, the societal changes that inevitably result from these periods in history can force consumers to reflect deeply on their own values and, by extension, their relationships and loyalty to the brands they use.

If you are in step with these changes, you have the Power of Ten on your side—yours is an Innovator Brand. If you choose to remain on the sidelines, out of fear or simply inertia, your brand will sink toward Quo Brand status.

Recently, there have been a spate of rebrands in the media industry, as legacy print publications continue to decline into Quo status and even some darlings of the digital age marry, divorce, change their names, and move to a different state, as it were. Verizon Communications merged its household-name acquisitions AOL and Yahoo! into a company nobody has ever heard of, called Oath. Even venerable Time Inc. has recently been pondering a rebrand, but the Power of Ten is not on its side. Decades of complacency and a failure to grasp the changing needs and habits of consumers has left Time scrambling for market share and grasping at any straw that will lend the brand greater relevancy. *TIME* magazine has even considered changing its name to *Life*, the title of the great mid-century photojournalism publication. But is adopting the fifty-plus-year-old name of a defunct print publication leveraging the Power of Ten, or is it actually diminishing the brand by x^{-5}?

Tribune Publishing, parent company of the *Los Angeles Times* and the *Chicago Tribune*, found itself in a similar bind and tried to leap over several decades of moribund strategic thinking in a single bound by renaming itself Tronc. This prompted a tide of derision from media critics who felt the companies were making rash, ill-advised branding moves instead of addressing the larger problem of having rested on one's laurels for half a century. As Twitter user @jontalton put it, "Sign of a new dark age when a grand name like Tribune is replaced by Tronc." *(For further discussion on this topic, please refer to the chapter "The Power of Eight.")*

As the Baby Boomers head into the sunset, they'll be taking a couple of brands with them unless the leadership of those brands finds a way to achieve relevance with younger generations. Harley-Davidson has been on the decline, losing 17% in sales in 2017. Similarly, rock-and-roll stalwarts Fender and Gibson are in decline, with sales dropping 33% in the last decade, according to *The Washington Post*. In a world where the new generation is listening to synth, dub step, rap, and the custom mixes of DJs, "There are no more guitar heroes."

In 2008, the Great Recession slammed the economies of the world and drained consumer spending power as households went into defensive mode. The Cadillac Escalade and the brawny Hummer, which had been emblematic of the "bling" and swagger of the previous decade, suddenly looked grotesque, while the thrifty Ford Focus and eminently practical Taurus enjoyed newfound popularity among the sobered middle class. GM went bankrupt, and when it reemerged, gone were the hulking SUVs. Leading the reinvention of the brand was the Chevy Volt, an electric hybrid vehicle. The Chevrolet logo had changed, too, displaying a greater degree of dimensionality and more solid lines that telegraphed strength and resolve. The macho "Chevy Runs Deep" slogan was replaced with the hopefully optimistic "Find New Roads."

Fast-forward to 2017, and the SUVs are on steroids once again as a record bull market pumps up the value of stock portfolios and the record production of energy, encouraged by the widespread availability of fracking technology, has driven gasoline prices ever lower. Yet at the same time, sales of hybrids and electric vehicles to the climate conscious segment of the market are at an all-time high. You have to give the car companies credit—they certainly have learned to read the tea leaves of consumer sentiment with great skill.

This points to a definite reality, that consumer brands probably will need a refresh somewhat more often than business-to-business brands. But one of the biggest mistakes we see is for the leadership of B2B brands to de-prioritize branding to the point that decades can pass before some rude awakening or sudden reputational issue shines a spotlight on just how much the brand has deteriorated, along with its strength and value.

Facing the Difficult Truth

Around the same time as the banks were failing and Chevy was struggling, we were retained by a leading specialty insurance company to help it find its own "new road." This carrier provided professional liability insurance to certified public accountants, many of whom were facing claims in the wake of the huge financial losses suffered by their clients. Now, if the combination of insurance and accounting sounds *doubly* boring to you, we can safely say that this project was anything but. A good brand and culture strategy can make anything exciting.

As these claims began to mount, the insurer's leaders realized the looming disaster if they didn't take action on the business front as well as the brand and culture front. A ratings downgrade was imminent, which would leave the company exposed to competitors looking to poach policyholders. The talent within the carrier would begin to feel insecure about their jobs, and could begin seeking other employment opportunities. This leadership team knew it could handle the business side of the equation, but sought our counsel on the brand and culture component.

Not unlike many specialized business-to-business operations, the company had not changed its corporate identity since it was founded in the mid-80s, and in the face of this crisis, the logo, website, advertising, and all other expressions of the brand suddenly looked very tired and potentially incapable of dealing with the crisis. We convened the key stakeholder group, solicited their confidential and anonymous insights through an online portal we had built, and brought our analysis of those insights to open a one-day brand strategy workshop. At this workshop, we facilitated as the stakeholders discussed, came to consensus behind collaboratively-crafted statements, then edited these until they said the most with the least number of words, and finally codified all the components of a brand and culture strategy into a concise and immediately actionable framework.

With this strategic framework in hand, we proceeded to update all the creative expressions of the brand, from the logo to the website through to the advertising and tradeshow presence. The rebrand was launched only a few weeks after the ratings downgrade, and served as a counterweight that neutralized competitor initiatives to steal policyholders, and as a morale booster that calmed any jitters the workforce may have had. In the end, the talent stood by the company as did the customers: The renewal rate at the end of the year was 96%, just one or two percentage points fewer than in a typical year.

It's important to note that while this is a good example of how a rebrand can help organizations weather a crisis, it might not have been necessary to make such an extraordinary and reactive effort had the company been regularly exercising the Power of Ten.

Other Triggers of a Rebrand

Internal events, such as a change in leadership or ownership, often trigger discussion of rebranding. In these cases, the rebrand clearly is designed to telegraph the strength and intentions of the new leadership. This signals to customers that their loyalty is not only safe, but will be rewarded even more in the form of better service and newer, more innovative products; and for investors in the brand, higher share prices and bigger dividends. Often, it is a new CEO or CMO who will come in and "clean house," bringing successful strategies from their last job, or perhaps some unrealized visions from that tenure, and putting them into practice at their new post.

This was the case when the VP of Marketing for a technology company named SPS Inc. came to us. She explained that the new CEO was eager to elucidate a new brand vision that would attract investors, customers, and talent to the company. The initials in the name stood for "Strategic Polymer Solutions," which totally failed to convey just how exciting the company's technology really was. The product was a thin-film polymer which, when exposed to a digital electric signal, could vibrate, change shape, play music, and so on. When deformed (pressed by a finger or vibrated by sound), it would also generate its own digital electric signal. In other words, this made it possible to send the sense of touch over the Internet. So if a parent were traveling on business, for instance, they could kiss their kids goodnight by kissing the screen of their phone while the kid pressed theirs to their cheek. "SPS Inc." simply didn't capture the magic of it all.

We went through our strategy development process with the key stakeholders of the company. This resulted in a comprehensive brand strategy that featured a powerful new vision for the company and how its ground-breaking technology would usher in a whole new era. We were even able to coin a new phrase for this era—the "Neo-Sensory Age." To this day, if you Google that phrase, this company will come up. But it won't come up under the SPS Inc. moniker. The strategy also yielded a new name for the company—Novasentis—to help it convey the wonder and potential of the brand and its products. This transformation would never had happened if the new CEO and his marketing VP hadn't spearheaded this effort. As we often say, branding takes guts.

Six Signs You're Ready for a Brand Refresh

Leadership must clearly understand, embrace and communicate a brand direction for their firms. When is it time to develop or reconsider a strategy?

Sometimes there are obvious *reactive* reasons. For instance, you want to maintain market share even when confronted with perceived smaller and weaker competitors. Rebranding provides an opportunity to focus on your commitment to the clients. Or how about bad PR? That can be the death of a brand. Finding a new way to present your company gives your client base an opportunity to rediscover your positive attributes. Finally, you may face legal issues. There are a number of reasons to rebrand for legal reasons; trademarks are most common.

Ah, but being *proactive* is a whole different story. This requires reflection, a bit of pride-swallowing, and action. Some clues you might be ready for a proactive brand refresh:

1. You're taking your people for granted.

Brand and culture are intertwined. One simply cannot be strengthened without the other. Are your employees coming to work only because they have to? They'll be uninspired, and far less productive, than their cohorts at innovator brands. Listen to your ambassadors. Remember your "why"—why is everyone here at this firm anyway? What is the better world or state of affairs you're trying to achieve?

2. You're basking.

Success can breed complacency. It may not be readily apparent, but the factors that landed customers and revenue in the last ten years likely will be drastically altered over the next ten. That's why well-run companies have their feet on the gas, even in down times— effectively looking out the windshield, not the rear-view mirror. They're paranoid about the brand. They question. They experiment. They take risks. They say, "If it ain't broke, break it."

3. Your place feels like a rummage sale.

It's obviously time for a refreshed brand strategy for firms facing a merger or acquisition. But other times you just accumulate various assets and then have to wrestle with them.

A brand strategy process will ask the right questions about the business . . . and answer them. If you follow that up with the development of a well-structured brand architecture, the company will have a clear roadmap for growth through brand extensions, and customers will have a clear idea of how all your different products and offers work together and relate to each other, easing the cross-selling process.

Sometimes a corporate event will prompt the need for a strategic review of the brand. That could take the form of a merger, acquisition, loss of a key customer, financial pressure, or drop in stock price.

But most times there isn't one obvious event driving a need for a refreshed brand and culture strategy. What if you've simply accumulated a series of sub-brands or introduced products and services that aren't cleanly connected in identity or culture? In that case, more actually is less.

Let's say you just moved into a new house. The garage is fairly empty at that point. But a few years later, what happens? The garage is where stuff that used to be in the house goes—and the future of that stuff isn't very promising. The next stop is a charitable donation, rummage sale, or the curb.

One of our clients amassed twenty-six different subsidiaries and programs. The costs of maintaining that many distinct brands was significant. The brand marks looked nothing alike in terms of tone, font color, or personality. When we put them all together on a sheet of paper, the result was quite striking—and not in a good way. The cleanup process is now under way.

Even innovative brands get into trouble with this. In their exuberant or frenetic growth, they'll launch new services or absorb weaker competitors. Many times the owners of these divisions will freelance with brand and culture. Here, for example, you might see the cultural clash of "Wild West" vs. staid, old-fashioned thinking.

When companies merge or acquire other companies, rebranding is often required to help employees and clients better understand what the company is and how they are there to help them. This does not always mean the parent company brand takes precedence. Best practices ensure the culture and brand is revisited. Again, the signal to the marketplace is that the new entity is not only bigger, but better as well.

A methodical brand strategy process will ask the right questions about the growth and positioning of the business and its culture—and answer them.

For example:

- Will you be a branded house (Virgin) or a house of brands (GM)? Many firms are somewhere in the middle, unsure of themselves. You've got to keep the story clean and easy for your target prospects and customers to understand.
- What will be the standard operating practice going forward as you acquire or build subsidiaries, operating units, programs, etc.? A plan here will stop arguments and the reinvention of wheels—saving you time and money in the long run.
- Who will serve as your brand police to prevent the dumping of stuff in the garage? While every worker has responsibilities here, the overall leadership mantle must be championed by one individual, one department, or one unified team. Be always vigilant!

4. You're "too busy."

Like a child tinkering with toys, is your firm moving from one ultimately unsuccessful tactic to another? Is strategy exhausting to think about? Innovator firms develop a strategy that optimizes every aspect of their brands, using multiple touchpoints to engage with customers and partners to build loyalty. Every contact reinforces the brand promise. Every piece of messaging—from the way phones are answered, to the elevator pitch, to the website, to the way the office looks and functions, to the LinkedIn updates—is tied directly to the lexicon of the brand strategy.

5. You're feeling stale.

When a company detects slipping relevancy in the minds of its customers, prospects, and talent, a rebrand can bring new energy.

Maybe it's been eight or ten years since you've looked at your brand and culture strategy—assuming you even have a strategy that has been written down and shared with employees. Are the words, such as your core values, still relevant?

The identity (name, logo, tagline) is the physical manifestation of the brand, which is the intangible set of expectations and memories that reside in the minds of all stakeholders. Ask: "If this brand identity were an employee, is it pulling its weight for this firm?" If the answer is "no" or "not sure," consider an employee evaluation—and maybe a firing. Moreover, that process should trigger a broader, strategic, forward-thinking look at the brand. Traces of stale pieces could be everywhere. How about Times New Roman font on your website?

6. You're predicting growth or new lines of business.

When a company is preparing for expected growth, it might rebrand products and services into a consolidated brand for consistency and to save money over time. This is also done when a company needs to create a greater sense of brand unity across different lines of business.

When a company enters a new line of business or market that is not cohesive to its existing brand identity, it's time for reflection. How about the need to appear to a new audience? This might not require an actual name or logo change, but rather a way to broaden the brand to target a new demographic.

Often it just comes down to the obvious: A new CEO may wish to elucidate a new vision for the company, and seeks to engage customers and the workforce in this new vision.

The brand is like a house. A fresh coat of paint will look nice for a while. That's a tactic. But consider the foundation and the framing underneath the paint: Are they weak or even crumbling? Addressing those is strategy.

When it's time, firms must go through a thoughtful process of defining and codifying brand attributes and personality. What are those brand elements today? With the proper strategy and investment, what *should* and *will* they be?

Tony's Take: The Decades in Every Cup of Peet's Coffee

I can still remember my very first cup of Peet's Coffee, at the original Peet's storefront in Berkeley, California. Yes, it's a little strange to remember such a thing, but that just goes to show how a remarkable customer experience can cement a brand image for life.

It was a lovely spring day, and after a few months of wandering around the country with all my worldly possessions packed into an old Chevy Suburban, I had stopped in Berkeley on what I had expected to be just a short layover before continuing up the coast to Seattle. My brother, Joe, took me around to see the town, showing me the UC campus, stopping in for lunch at Chez Panisse, surveying the astonishing variety of foods in all the markets, and then, that fateful walk over to Peet's.

A somewhat-motley crew of aging hippies congregated outside, one sitting on a worn wooden bench, playing a mandolin while others sang, read poetry, and conversed passionately about politics and social issues—almost as if it were staged for a coffeehouse scene in a movie. Inside it was all dark-stained wood, with bins full of beans labeled with intriguing names such as "Major Dickason's Blend" and the whirring of the coffee grinders rising above the soft hubbub of the sizable crowd of customers. A most fantastic scent of coffee wafted through the air in invisible sheets.

I ordered a large black coffee from an aproned employee whom I had previously heard having a passionate, in-depth conversation with another customer about the perfect level of grind for a particular type of coffee maker. "You might want to go with a small to start," Joe said to me, dipped his chin down and cocked an eyebrow. "This is some very strong coffee." I scoffed at him. After all, I had been in Ann Arbor at the University for years prior to this journey—I was a veteran chugger of "strong" coffee. How could this be any different?

Well, it *was* different. Not only was the flavor rich and complex beyond anything I had ever tasted before, it was without a doubt the strongest coffee I had ever had in my entire life up to that point. Not only did I resort to putting milk in it (highly unusual for me), but I was only about halfway through this large cup when my hands started to shake and a sweat broke out on my forehead. I couldn't finish the whole thing, I was so over-caffeinated. I was also impressed. This was a whole new experience for me, and despite having the jitters for the rest of the day, I would be back the next morning for more; I also unpacked the truck that afternoon, knowing that Northern California was my kind of place.

I've been a Peet's guy ever since, even though the benches and the hippies are gone, and the coffee they make these days is not quite as strong as it was at that original Berkeley store. That was in 1989, but Peet's didn't really become a national brand until recently. By 2000 it had become a regional player, and another ten years later a series of acquisitions allowed it to expand across the U.S. Each step of the way, the brand image became more refined, and the product became a little more mainstream (but definitely not generic). Peet's puts the Power of Ten in every cup it serves.

Peter's Take: AIG or Chartis?

Many decades ago, American International Group was founded. Well, that was a long and vague name—although the term "international" was hip back in those days. And since no one could or would write or say "American International Group" every time, AIG was born—probably starting on internal documents written by top exec Maurice "Hank" Greenberg himself, then with regulatory agencies, then clients, then on the world stage. Hundreds of millions of advertising dollars later, AIG was a top insurance brand.

Fast-forward to the 2007-2008 financial crisis, and "AIG" had acquired a stench, as they say here in Washington's political circles. So in 2009, the replacement name "Chartis" was introduced. But then the company announced a change back to AIG. And now there's a refreshed, brighter AIG logo to go with it all.

If we could go back in time, why wouldn't Chartis be the original moniker? Chartis actually means something. It's derived from "map" in Greek. Charting the way. Following a clear road map. Demonstrating leadership. These are all delightful things around which to build brand experiences.

Again, I dislike initials for brand names. I'm on a mission to stomp them out. Most of them sound like a fungus or some awful disease you get on your upper lip.

I didn't take my own medicine, originally. Launched in 1999, marketing-communications firm The van Aartrijk Group was a mouthful to say. We started internally, then externally, writing "TVAG" or "VAG."

Ugh.

We subsequently refreshed our brand name as "Aartrijk" (pronounced "R-trike," as in bike). I realize that's challenging because it's a phonetic exception in English, but the word actually means something in Dutch—"kingdom of fertile soil."

In sum, my advice:

Unless you have an AIG-style bucket of money for global branding, resist the temptation to take the easy way out by relying on acronyms for firms, programs, projects, products or services. Take the extra time to craft a name using a couple of words or phrases that actually *mean* something. Acronyms typically do not; that's why, for example, the National Association of Realtors isn't "NAR." The organization opted for Realtors. The members are real people, not vague entities from the planet Nar.

There are lots of mergers in financial services. Everyone wants their initials in the original acronyms to survive. Make the tough decision to avoid combining letters to create . . . yes, yet another acronym.

If you must keep any acronyms, choose those that actually say—and *stand for*—something. NetVU and ASCnet are two examples. They are *networks* of users of technology. "VU" is the vision to the future. "ASC" refers to leveraging talented peers, which is reinforced in the organization's tagline, "Ask us."

If you still need evidence of why my rant is warranted, talk with customers and business partners about what *your* letters and acronyms mean to them. You'll be surprised over the confusion.

Are you proceeding carefully with those letters, my friends? Or are you getting lost in the soup?

THE POWER OF NINE

Successful brands are
always dressed to the nines.

"Focus on building the best possible business. If you are great, people will notice and opportunities will appear."
—Mark Cuban

"**D**ressed to the nines" is an old-fashioned term for someone who has paid attention to every detail of their outfit and is dressed to perfection. Legend has it that the term comes from the 99th (Lanarkshire) Regiment of Foot, a British infantry unit known for its smart uniforms.

For the retail brand Target, it means a clean, smart, simple logo and aisles filled with Philippe Starck toilet brushes, Method soap, and Missoni apparel. These designer elements lend what would otherwise be just another Walmart wannabe the cache of cool it needs to compete against other general retailers.

The Sephora brand is a great example of how the Power of Nine can provide an advantage. Traditionally, cosmetics were sold either in the plebeian, fluorescent-lit aisles of drugstores or the stuffy, upscale halls of major department stores. The drugstores had good prices but didn't have the upscale products or knowledgeable salespeople, while the department stores only carried the high-end stuff, which came with a generous dose of snooty, high-pressure sales tactics from the staff. Neither option provided a wide range of choices.

Walk into a Sephora store (or visit their online version) and you'll get the Goldilocks experience—everything is just right. The displays are colorful and dazzling, set against a backdrop of stark, glossy black and white. There is every product imaginable, and knowledgeable, almost exceedingly energetic and friendly associates roam the aisles, eager to help. The prices are good. The air is perfumed. The people watching is brilliant. (The place is always packed. Always.) This brand shines with the Power of Nine.

Apple. From the happening scene in the retail stores with nerd-chic hipster "Geniuses" to the exquisite packaging that makes you feel like a six-year-old on Christmas morning, every aspect of this brand—whether it's the logo, the website, or the brilliant products themselves—every silicon atom of this brand shimmers with the Power of Nine. Hard to imagine that it was dismissed as a stylish but hopelessly impractical computer company at one point, as now it represents luxury-tech. Steve Jobs was famous for obsessing over the details of the Apple brand—from the products to the stores, to the "spaceship" corporate headquarters—and it really, really shows.

For a brand to leverage the Power of Nine, every customer touchpoint has to be considered, whether that's in the brick-and-mortar world or the digital environment.

Ray Kroc was not above getting down on his hands and knees to scrape gum off the floor of a McDonald's he was visiting, all in the pursuit of the Power of Nine. Whether all McDonald's franchisees share that same commitment in today's world is questionable, but there's no doubt the Power of Nine helped the brand achieve great success.

Clearly, this commitment to strive for perfection can't be limited to CEOs. Every member of the team has to be clear on the core tenets of the brand and aligned behind the overall strategy in order to deliver the Power of Nine. There is a famous story of President John F. Kennedy visiting NASA. While there, he stopped to chat with a janitor and asked him what he was working on. "I'm helping put a man on the moon," the janitor is said to have answered as he cleaned the floor. That's a great example of clarity and alignment behind a brand, and a belief in the Power of Nine.

Google's ability to deliver all the world's knowledge instantaneously is almost taken for granted at this point, but it's the result of the world's best minds ceaselessly improving the complex code that drives its search algorithm. The brand also did something remarkable at the time it was launched: The web page, unlike all the other complex, visually-crowded "web portals" of the time, was completely minimalist. Only the logo, the search box, and the choice between a regular search or the intriguing "I Feel Lucky" selection. After that novelty wore off, the marketing team would have the logo occasionally morph, usually to honor a significant day (something that was invented, an important milestone in humanity, the birthday of a famous person), providing an appropriate injection of whimsy or reflection into what would otherwise have been a prosaic search function. Even today, now that Alphabet is the holding company and the Google brand represents only the search function, its identity has matured to a clean, bright, orderly, sans serif logo. Its sister companies (AdWords, Waymo, etc.) all have similarly elegant identities. The entire family is "dressed to the nines."

The guilty pleasure of eating a still-warm Krispy Kreme donut is made *that much better* by watching it get made right before your eyes by an incredible Rube Goldberg of a machine, handed to you by a cheerful, nattily-uniformed associate, and then devouring it in an environment of sparklingly clean, tiled surfaces. The Power of Nine never tasted so sweet.

Behind the impressive silver facade, Tiffany may represent the epitome of the Power of Nine. Not just because of the glittering array of exquisitely-designed jewelry displayed under a billion sparkling points of light, but also because of the familiarity of its signature sky-blue box.

When you're managing all your brand touchpoints so they exceed the customer's expectations and cause unexpected delight, that's the Power of Nine.

The Power of Nine vs. the Fountain of Eternal Youth

When you think of great wine regions of the world, what comes to mind? In the U.S., Napa is at the top, having been put on the map in the late 1970s in a famous taste test, known as the "Judgement of Paris," when the upstarts from the New World bested the finest, most-pedigreed wines of France.

Are Millennials digging Napa? Let's just say it's not a monogamous relationship. Sometimes they are drawn to the less-fancy, more down-to-earth grape growers in neighboring Sonoma, which conveys an authentic farming feel for these urban dwellers. Or down south in the Golden State to Monterey or Simi, or other relatively newer wine-growing valleys. In Europe, Rioja in Spain, Chianti in Italy, and Bordeaux in France. Maybe you like those beautiful shiraz wines from Barossa Valley in Australia. Or perhaps you're intrigued by the small producers of South Africa's Stellenbosch region.

Millennials are also increasingly drawn to hip startup wineries in Baja. (Yep, Mexico.) And all fifty states produce wine—we won't argue here about how good or bad some of it is—and people today are obsessed with the terms craft, new, startup, community, David (vs. Goliath), quirky, and artsy.

Napa achieved perfect Power of Nine status, but only in the eyes of Boomers. How can the valley and its winery champions transform themselves? Can they? Do they need to? This is why you need to keep evolving, because there's always someone thinking of a better way and resonating in a way you never thought possible. The Napa winemaking elite, having beaten the best of the best, would never have thought they'd be facing competition from popups in Baja.

As times change, Napa risks becoming old hat, losing its Power of Nine as the dust settles in. Don't believe it could ever happen? Look at Atlantic City, New Jersey, which was the inspiration for the game Monopoly and was the number one resort destination in the country up until the Great Depression and World War II changed the tenor of the country's mood.

If you're not a wine lover, the same thing is unfolding before our very eyes with food trucks, craft beer, and spirits, isn't it? These new products look great, with a whole new appeal to a whole new kind of consumer: The Millennials, a huge generation that is a third larger than Boomers, are calling the shots.

If you don't have the Power of Ten, and you're not dressed to the Nines, you might find yourself behind the Eight Ball. And we'll address that next.

Tony's Take: Nine Brands That Are Dressed to the Nines

Of course, beauty is always in the eye of the beholder, but these are nine decades-old brands I admire for having done a perfect job of consistently reinventing themselves to meet the changing needs of their target audience and their workforce, all while looking great at the same time:

- Apple: The combination of cool design and pure pragmatism is downright sexy.
- Volvo: The perfect balance of safety and luxury as only the Scandinavians can do.
- Bang & Olufsen: The sound of perfection is so subtle it's deafening.
- Ben & Jerry's: Now, and probably forever, the king of quirky desserts.
- IKEA: Swedish meatballs and flat-pack shelving all under the same bright blue and yellow roof.
- Starbucks: Not the absolute greatest coffee in the world, but could civilized society survive without it at this point? This brand fills our need for a "Third Place" perfectly.
- Lego: The plastic building blocks that today's grandparents played with as children are still as relevant and popular as ever.
- HBO: Anticipating—nay, driving—entertainment trends since 1972. Competitors? They all eventually get "whacked."

- Nike: It started out selling shoes, but now sells existential existence. And it does it with an athletic grace and power that is unmatched.

THE POWER OF EIGHT

Don't get behind the eight ball.

"Pay attention to your enemies, for they are the first to discover your mistakes."

—**Antisthenes**, Greek philosopher

P ool players know that when you're "behind the eight ball," it generally means you're in some sort of trouble, usually due to some mishandling of a situation. You failed to think ahead, or you didn't execute properly. Brands find themselves in such spots from time to time, sitting on their laurels, complacent. And it takes some clever maneuvering to get out from behind the dreaded black orb.

Look to Microsoft for a perfect example. The brand that became synonymous with computer software clearly did not see the approaching convergence of increased computing power, miniaturization, and the Internet, and failed to create neither an ecosystem to manage this convergence, nor a brand that could naturally adopt it. Apple clearly did, and was at the right place at the right time with the right products, namely the iPod, the iPhone, and the iPad. Microsoft stumbled to play catch-up, launching the feature-laden Zune music player five years after the iPod. It landed with a resounding thud. Add the failed but feature-laden Vista and the features-bloated Windows Mobile operating systems and any number of misguided products, such as the original Surface PixelSense coffee table (a pinball machine-size piece of furniture containing a glass-surfaced touch computer that did the same thing as an iPhone, only couldn't fit in your pocket, let alone most apartments), and Microsoft suddenly found itself falling behind Apple in nearly every way, especially in terms of brand value. Microsoft had fallen under the Power of Eight, and no amount of additional features could help it.

Getting behind the eight ball, or falling under the Power of Eight, is not necessarily the end of a brand unless it turns into a death spiral of bad strategies followed by unwise investments. In Microsoft's case, it seems they may be rescued by the arrival of a new CEO, Satya Nadella, whose style is more curious and nuanced than the pugnacious Steve Ballmer, whom he succeeded in 2014.

Death of a Brand: A Saab Story

The Saab automobile brand suffered this fate and, unfortunately, there was no Nadella-like CEO to come riding in and save it from itself. First, the company alarmed the faithful when, as the result of a cost-cutting chassis platform partnership with Fiat, Lancia, and Alfa Romeo, it released the Saab 9000, a whaleboat of a car with—gasp!—the ignition on the steering column, instead of the uniquely

Saab positioning on the floor between the seats, where it had resided for three decades. Also because of this so-called "Platform Four," the cars from each of the brands looked remarkably similar, diluting the iconoclastic and cutting-edge design previously attributed to Saab. This brand betrayal was compounded further when Saab management sold half the company to GM, which mainstreamed the look of the vehicles even more as they marketed the car to a broader segment of the population. These missteps tarnished the brand's cache and brought about the exodus of its core constituency.

The 2009 U.S. government takeover of GM and subsequent restructuring required the sale of Saab, which was purchased by the Dutch custom-luxury manufacturer Spyker. This could have been the brand's saving grace, but it was so deep under the Power of Eight at this point that the new owners did not have the financial resources to resurrect the old Saab mystique (let alone its production line). Saab fell into bankruptcy and was picked apart by creditors by the end of 2011.

Imagine if Saab, prior to its acquisition by GM, had revisited its brand strategy and discovered that "independent," "individual," "quirky," and "rebellious" were inextricable parts of its DNA that could not be ignored? Would "Platform Four" have never happened? Would the leadership have perhaps chosen a better partner, say, Fiat, or VW, instead of GM? A solid brand strategy often can be the guiding light for sound management decisions, and keep the organization from falling under the Power of Eight.

The High-Stakes Celebrity Pool Game

Celebrity endorsements are a double-edged sword for brands. When the celebrity is hot and you're slicing the competition into prosciutto, life is good. When the celebrity trips and the brand falls on that sword—well, not so good.

The foibles of even the most upright-seeming celebrities are eventually exposed and magnified by social media and the Internet; association with stars is a minefield for brands. Eventually someone's going to step in it.

Gone are the days of the actor Robert Young and his genteel TV physician persona, Marcus Welby, M.D., pitching for Sanka decaffeinated coffee. In this modern world of ours, someone probably would have dug up dirt on the poor fellow and sunk Sanka in the process. But back then it was pretty easy to maintain a facade, as Hollywood and the media largely worked together to control a celebrity's images. SoMe has destroyed this concept, putting the power of the press in the hands of anyone with a mobile phone. And that would be pretty much everyone.

People love celebrity success stories. And while most won't admit it, we also get equal enjoyment from seeing those same stars fall from the heavens they inhabit. When it comes to brands and celebrity endorsements, these actors, sports heroes, and rock stars can leave quite a bit of carnage as they go down in flames,

The landscape is dotted with examples. Accenture couldn't quite endure the foibles of golf champion Tiger Woods as he crashed cars, over-helped himself to prescription (or other) drugs, met some ladies along the way, and got into a messy, and very public, domestic dispute with his wife.

What was Subway to do when their "everyday Joe," Jared Fogle, the fellow who famously downsized his waistline with the Subway Diet and coincidentally upsized revenues for the fast-food chain, was busted for possession of child pornography? A quick check on Google shows they are going to have a hard time putting any significant distance between the brand and the bad boy.

Some brands go with multiple celebrities to mitigate the danger of a large, long-term investment in a single character. Big car insurance companies GEICO and Progressive have their stars (e.g. Flo) but they have backups such as cavemen, basketballs, talking boxes, and other cartoon figures. GEICO's gecko can't switch sides, but what would happen if Flo switched to State Farm? Ask Sprint and Verizon. "Can you hear me now?" pitchman Paul Marcarelli switched from Verizon to Sprint the moment his contract/non-compete was up.

Tour de France champion Lance Armstrong turned out to have some issues with doping that made certain brands look like dopes, as well. While rumors of illegal performance-enhancing drugs had swirled around him for decades, brands still took their chances and signed him on to hawk their products. Once the indisputable truth really came out, his endorsement empire quickly fell apart as Anheuser-Busch, Trek, BRG Sports (formerly Easton-Bell Sports), 24-Hour Fitness, Honey Stinger, Oakley, and other brands that should have known better beat a hasty retreat. Nike was livid. The U.S. Postal Service was dismayed. But no one should have been surprised.

Even the great ad man David Ogilvy eventually swore off celebrity endorsements. Not because of scandal, but because consumers regularly remembered the star but couldn't recall the product. After all, did you head down to the post office more often because you wanted to catch the scintillating essence of Lance Armstrong that hung in the air as you waited in those interminable lines? Did you send your packages Priority Mail instead of Parcel Post, because the prestige of the Tour de France rubbed off on the recipient?

If we can say anything for celebrity endorsements, it's that they have to be relevant. For Nike, Lance Armstrong was a good fit. For the USPS? OK, speedy service. Except everyone knows the post office isn't speedy. OK, um, grit and determination. Except we've all experienced the mind-numbing lines and poor service, so not making the connection there, either. There really does have to be *some* alignment between the celebrity and the brand.

In the end, association with a celebrity is a bit like timing the market. You have to end the relationship as it's rising, and not hold on until the inevitable slide begins. That's as hard for the average house-flipper and day trader, trying to maximize profits before the market turns, as it is for CMOs who enjoy the perks of being hitched to a rising star. The strongest brands are bigger than any pitchman anyway.

You have to understand the risk. If you make a superstar out of your pitchman, get out while the getting is good, or you could find your brand way behind the eight ball and all over the front pages of the tabloids.

Digital Transformation Complicates Things

The Power of Eight has become especially important since brands such as Google, Amazon, Uber, and Netflix have come to define the customer experience through their absolute mastery of digital transformation. If you're trying to compete with them directly, well, good luck with that. But even if you don't consider companies such as these competitors, they have set the baseline expectations and your firm, whether you're in banking or cupcakes, is competing with these digital experience expectations and is going to have to meet those expectations in the delivery of the digital side of your business.

According to digital marketing agency Ciceron, 90% of consumers note that their purchase decisions are influenced by online reviews. Technology analyst Gartner reports that 67% of the buyer's journey generally involves a digital component. So as your customers routinely come to expect a better journey facilitated by technology, and you routinely deny them that convenience, the more your brand will fall in Quo territory. When a brand falls behind in technology, its reputation reflects that reality. How often have you heard someone say about a brand, "They used to be really great at *x*, but lately they've really been slipping." These days, you hear that most in regards to the digital experience. But especially if your business is a local, regional, or highly-specialized player, being able to claim the best digital experience as part of your Brand Evidence is a big part of staying out in front of the eight ball. Make the investment—painful as it may seem.

How to Slip Behind the Eight Ball

Let's take a look at some common issues we have observed:

1. **Self-serving brand vision that will corrupt you.**

Reality check: Vision statements should not be about you or your company. That can be a difficult concept to grasp for left-brained, rational thinkers in the C-suite who, even though they have good intentions, can hamper a firm's brand and culture by focusing on corporate financial goals as faux vision statements. If the vision isn't about a happier place for your customers, or even the world, you won't achieve your full potential. Macy's kiss-kiss-on-us vision statement starts like this: "[A] premier omnichannel retailer with iconic brands that serve customers through outstanding stores, dynamic online sites, and mobile apps." It sure looks like customers have been voting with their feet on this business plan masked as a vision.

2. Losing sight of core values.

For firms in the unfortunate position of having to recall consumer goods, there is always one proper choice. Did Firestone make the right one on its flawed tires? Probably not. Did Johnson & Johnson get out from behind the eight ball when it learned its Tylenol was being laced with deadline cyanide? Definitely yes. Ask the millions of moms who came back to Tylenol in droves when J&J recalled all its product and introduced tamper-evident packaging. Here's a costly short-term decision that has returned gazillions to shareholders by management paying attention to core values. Don't mess with families or family safety.

3. Ego and hubris.

Have you seen the brooding, dark 2015 Super Bowl ad by Nationwide? Any amount of consumer pre-testing surely would have suggested that a dead kid as a spokesperson would be a buzz-kill bust for a fun venue like a football game. Only Nationwide's resident CMO at the time would defend it.

4. Lack of focus on customer's deep human needs.

Local car dealerships can succeed at various levels, but they're always about some sort of sales job. Set your advertising clock by it: President's Day, Memorial Day, Fourth of July, Labor Day, year-end . . . The latest sales promotion is just an exuberant, if not screaming, spokesperson away. The wary customer finally gets a car and is asked to fill out a satisfaction survey so the salesperson and dealership can earn—you guessed it—more commission at the end of the year. "Please give us 10s!" they say. You leave with your car—maybe even your dream car—but you feel like you need a shower to wash off the shameful behavior. ("Let me check with my manager and see if we can do that rust protection for free.") Meanwhile, CarMax buys and sells cars, just like dealers. They pay commissions. They ultimately may even charge more in most cases, who knows. But why is the customer experience so different? CarMax has tapped into the deep human needs of car shoppers: maybe the need to not feel pressured, yes, and also the need for respect, pride, patience, individuality, etc. Cars are *things* you buy; people are seeking more.

5. Letting competitors own your brand.

Whether they like it or know it, or not, every organization faces competition. These can be primary, secondary, and dark-horse competitors. When the CEO of McDonald's declared at an annual shareholders' meeting that the fast-food chain didn't have any real competition, the stock went down. A year later, he was singing a different tune: "Not only do we have competition, but they're really good." The stock went up. One of those competitors was Subway. You can argue about the quality of the ingredients (and the downside of paid spokespersons), but Subway guy Jared Fogle ate Ronald McDonald's lunch as it expanded to the world's largest fast-food chain in terms of store outlets. And it redefined a whole new category of options beyond hamburgers. Are you defining your brand's direction by experimenting with ways to meet evolving consumer interests? Or are you drifting around in a red ocean, susceptible to pirates?

6. **Bad management.**

Or call it bad leadership. Bad ideas. Either way, it's bad, bad, bad. It's making wrong moves and finding yourself in a weak position on the pool table. These moves can destroy value so quickly. There's pivot, innovation, experimentation, and even some failure. And then there are senseless business decisions. Have you heard of a company called Baldwin-United? Here's a maker of fine pianos that borrowed heavily in the 1980s to be in the business of . . . wait for it . . . annuities! And annuities that paid high commissions to brokers and a higher interest rate than the company itself could earn. You couldn't make that one up, right? Bankruptcy proceedings were next on the docket for these wandering musicians from Cincinnati.

The Highway of Commerce Is Littered with Eights

Woolworths. AOL. Blockbuster. Kodak. Sears. JCPenney. Oldsmobile. Saturn. Maxwell House. Atari. The list of "Eighters" goes on and on.

We could probably write the branding equivalent of *War and Peace* with all the case studies of brands that have found themselves falling under the Power of Eight, and although one learns the most about success by studying failures, that would make for a very depressing book indeed. Instead, let's refocus on how brands can get things right, by being open to opportunity and taking a few risks. Let's take a look at what it takes to garner the Power of Seven.

Tony's Take: Innovate to Get Outside the Eight

On an evening not too long ago, I attended a seminar at UC Berkeley Haas School of Business, hosted by Professor Henry Chesbrough and featuring the wisdom of Ashish Chatterjee, a Global CPG R&D Executive with Procter & Gamble. As Ashish tells it, even mindful, brand-centric companies like P&G sometimes find themselves falling under the Power of Eight.

In this case, P&G was falling way behind in its product development pipeline. Projects were bogged down in red tape and endless iterations. Historically, 85-90% of innovation had been done in-house, a siloed and secretive approach that Ashish wryly noted had led P&G to be dubbed "Kremlin on the Ohio."

Fortuitously, because the company had innovation in its brand DNA, they knew that part of the solution lay in being more innovative about its own brand, especially when it came to dealing with "blind spots." In other words, they had to get over the "not invented here" roadblock, where if an idea wasn't generated by internal resources, it couldn't possibly be any good.

"We had to crack the Kremlin," Chatterjee proclaimed.

Crack it they did, through an "Open Innovation" approach they called Connect + Develop. It was a surprisingly simple revelation: P&G had 8,000 R&D staffers, a formidable brain trust to be sure. But the world has more than two million scientists and engineers working on the same challenges. Not leveraging this brain power did not make sense.

A.G. Lafley, then CEO and Chairman of the Board, announced the goal of acquiring 50% of innovation from the outside. This was revolutionary, but that's the kind of approach P&G needed, because in order to get newer, bigger ideas—fast—it required fresh blood and fresh thinking.

Ashish noted that although "Innovation has always been our lifeblood," the fact of the matter was "You cannot have open innovation without a clear, strong brand strategy. That is unequivocal." The P&G brand vision was subsequently refined to embrace this new approach: "Dedicated to Touching and Improving Lives."

So brand strategy became part of the solution: The Tide detergent brand was extended into retail, becoming Tide Dry Cleaners. Gillette's men's razors birthed The Art of Shaving customer experience shops. P&G partnered with Clorox to develop the deodorizer Febreze which, in addition to becoming a standalone success, also became an important "ingredient brand" in such products as Fresh Step kitty litter.

Peter's Take: CEOs, Do Your Job

I read with interest United Airlines CEO Oscar Munoz's mea culpa—an open letter to the public—regarding the passenger being injured and dragged off the plane in April 2017.

It was splendid prose.

Of note, Munoz said this: "It happened because our corporate policies were placed ahead of our shared values. Our procedures got in the way of our employees doing what they know is right."

We already had enough evidence that values trump manuals. This incident didn't need to happen. Companies go wrong when they publish complex rules for everything in the company—how to dress, how to precisely use the logo and colors, how to speak to customers (verbatim), when to arrive, when to leave, how to handle a dispute with your manager—rules that nobody really reads, let alone understands or follows intuitively.

The firms with thick manuals are siloed—nobody knows what anyone else is doing or why. Communications are on a "need to know" basis, so there is a toxic lack of transparency that breeds rumors. Business leaders are obsessed with competitors—both inside and outside the company—instead of with customers.

These often are lonely places, where managers and employees never speak one-on-one and there's not much fun or laughter.

Worse yet, they can be places where only certain people are allowed to come up with ideas and solutions. There are a lot of politics—badmouthing, backbiting, blaming. There's no clear path for advancement, no sense of meritocracy.

Even though those kinds of brands and cultures exist within some companies, that's not what people desire. They desire purpose. They desire growth. They admire quality. They want to help make the world a better place. That's why we at Chromium advocate "branding from the inside out."

Because when a company has a clear purpose and is values-driven, you don't need thick manuals for everything—people can operate, communicate, and make decisions in relation to the values. The result is more efficiency, more autonomy, more personal achievement. Leadership needs to uphold the values, but needn't micromanage individuals.

"As CEO, it's my responsibility . . . to redouble our efforts to put our customers at the center of everything we do," Munoz said in his open letter.

"Redouble our efforts" is a cliché, and it's the wrong approach. United should put improving the culture for its 87,000 employee-owners at the center of everything. The customers—and the brand—will be the better for it.

Don't believe it? Just ask Southwest Airlines. When a passenger wrote to former CEO Herb Kelleher complaining that a flight attendant had sung the safety message on her flight and that she would no longer be flying Southwest, he wrote a return letter of four words: "We will miss you."

If you want to connect employees and customers, don't use thick manuals and operating procedures. Let everyone operate by the true core values of the brand.

Running an airline obviously presents myriad challenges. But none except safety should trump brand and culture strategy or management.

And regardless of your industry, a CEO who leaves brand to marketing and culture to HR is abdicating her or his responsibilities.

Yes, as the top exec you'll make deals happen, examine financials, hire and fire, get in the weeds on technical things, and sit in meetings. But that's not the job. The job is to create and maintain a firm where employees are so engaged and energized to come to work that they willingly—hopefully, even zealously—embrace the customer experience.

While the passenger was being dragged off the plane—which obviously no one at United or the Chicago O'Hare police wanted to do—Munoz could well have been presiding over an important tactical meeting such as a decision to pre-buy fuel, or entering into a new contract to lease-back jet engines. Is effective fuel management a competitive advantage? Sure. But is it more important to have the CEO focused on such operational matters more than highly strategic assets such as brand and culture? Nope. For the $1,200 United saved by kicking that fellow off the plane so the crew member could ride, more than $1 billion in stock value was lost in the ensuing scandal.

CEOs, focus on the primary job. Don't get behind the eight ball.

THE POWER OF SEVEN

Make yours a lucky brand.

"Those people and businesses that are generally considered fortunate or luckier than others are usually also the ones that are prepared to take the greatest risks and, by association, are also prepared to fall flat on their faces every so often."
—Richard Branson

Twitter is lucky. The company happened to be in the right place at the right time, becoming a virtual mercenary army on the side of the people in the street battles against repressive governments in the "Arab Spring" of 2010.

Southwest Airlines seems lucky. The brand always seems to be there with optimism, humor, and great prices right when air travelers need good vibes and good deals the most. And in a tough business to work, SWA is lucky to attract flight attendants who genuinely seem happy most of the time, while those at unlucky airlines fake it.

Toyota sure is lucky. Their Prius hybrid caught the eye of the consumer when gas prices climbed above $4 per gallon in the late 2000s. The vehicles also were allowed into carpool lanes, which made others even more envious of them as their drivers zipped past the congestion. Celebrities were seen driving them, affording the brand some star status that increased the desire for association.

In his book, *The Luck Factor*, Dr. Richard Wiseman of the University of Hertfordshire in the United Kingdom studied the various personality attributes and habits of people who considered themselves either "lucky" or "unlucky." What he found, above all else, was that people who self-identified as lucky were curious folks—always on the lookout for opportunity, eager to meet new people, and always seemed to maintain a positive attitude. People who self-identified as unlucky, on the other hand, tended to dwell on their own supposed misfortune, spending a disproportionate amount of time looking at their own feet and in the process literally did not see opportunities that were right in front of them.

In one part of the study, Wiseman's subjects were given a route to walk and a destination at a coffee shop where they would meet the researcher. Along the route, several five-pound bank notes were randomly placed. The "unlucky" types arrived empty-handed, having seen nothing interesting and having spoken with no one. The "lucky" subjects arrived with a note or two in hand, full of stories of what they had seen and the interesting people they had met. The big difference between being lucky and unlucky? Keeping your eyes, minds, and hearts open to opportunity. This is the Power of Seven.

Uber has been pretty lucky, although they've stepped in it a few times along the way. Still, when a company has a vision for changing the very nature of mobility, remarkable things happen along the way.

Just ask the taxi industry, which had made ignoring the Power of Seven (plus basic good manners and minimally acceptable levels of personal hygiene) standard practice.

Is your brand lucky or unlucky? If your brand doesn't have a positive, almost altruistic, vision for the better world it will help create, it will miss opportunities that could be instrumental to its success. Why? Because being focused entirely on what's in front of you, namely making quarterly profit numbers or everyday tactical issues, takes your mind off the future and the steps required to get there. Certainly this does not mean that a company should ignore revenue generation and neglect mundane but essential daily business duties. But by putting those business essentials in the context of a higher purpose, every action is imbued with meaning and passion, and permission to take risks in the pursuit of that vision will have been implicitly given.

Perhaps you're a by-the-numbers, "only duty a corporation has is to its shareholders" kind of leader, and this hippy-dippy, New Age, feel-good stuff is all a load of hooey to you and your beloved shareholders. Well, okay then. Venerable management consulting firm McKinsey & Company happens to share our viewpoint, and has gone so far as to back it up with some interesting insights and statistics. The typical American view that vision, values, and community-building are distractions from the bottom line, which veteran consultant Dominic Barton and others have termed "short-termism," detracts measurably from performance. "Long-term capitalists," who follow a more Scandinavian and European approach to building and operating a business, investing significantly in both R&D as well as the broader stakeholder community, seem to do a whole lot better. Significantly so, clocking stronger fundamentals and performance

than short-termists over the last fifteen years. Fifteen. Years.
Without exception:

- Earnings: +36%
- Revenue: + 47%
- Market Cap: + $7B

Like those numbers? Get on the vision and values train, and your
brand could share in the proverbial jackpot these "lucky" brands have
stumbled upon.

Living the Brand

Brand values are vital in the pursuit of the Power of Seven. If the stated
values of a company don't expressly open the door to opportunity
and innovation, and don't elucidate something that the larger group
of brand stakeholders can share, then the brand will not be as "lucky"
as those that take a few risks.

At a bank marketing conference a couple of years ago, ING Bank
founder Arkadi Kuhlmann explained how he relished talking with
potential employees. "When I interview people, I always ask: 'What
is your calling? What are you passionate about? What's your cause?'
That's where the energy is."

Noting that the customers of ING (now owned by Capital One)
were called "savers," Kuhlmann said to prospective employees: "Do
you have a savings account? Do you save?" If the candidate did not
identify as being a "saver," they wouldn't get hired.

He went on to say, "If the people making the bread don't eat the
bread, they can't live the brand. We wanted an alignment of personal
values and brand values."

Look at everything the brand does—from recruiting to building a culture that is open to opportunity—and you'll create your own good luck just by sticking to your own knitting. That's the Power of Seven.

It doesn't matter what industry you're in—opportunities abound. For example, look at State Farm, which was willing to take the risk of insuring farmers while other companies turned up their noses at those "hayseeds" and their tractors. State Farm got "lucky," and as a result was able to build a brand and a network of agents, and now issues two or three of every ten car insurance policies, a total $215 billion market in the U.S.

So, what kind of culture is your brand creating? A lucky one, which harnesses the Power of Seven by being open to outside ideas and sharing internal discoveries? Or is it one that is becoming unlucky by insisting that only by working twelve-hour days and meeting steep revenue goals will the company succeed?

Nike became a Power of Seven brand by moving beyond their comfort zone, venturing into the world of tech and wearables with the Fitbit. Amazon became a Power of Seven brand by introducing Prime, promising millions of customers they could have whatever they wanted, whether that was groceries or movies, essentially when they wanted it. Why? Both of these companies could have gone on as they had been for years, selling the same old stuff in the same old way to the same (increasingly older) people. That's not how you harness the Power of Seven—that's how you find yourself trapped in the Power of Eight.

The Power of Seven can be scary if you think about things too much. Yes, think about things, but think about things in general terms as to how they will affect your brand. If you can pull it off, will the result be positive or negative? Once you understand the bigger picture, consider the Power of Seven vs. the Power of Eight, and then it should all make sense. After all, even AAA (the American Automobile Association) is envisioning a world where no one actually owns an automobile. They went there, and it is guaranteed to take them to good places.

Letting your brand and your culture occasionally take side streets, and even get a little lost: That's the Power of Seven.

Peter's Take: 20/20 Vision

Of the nine components of a brand and culture strategy, none is more important than the vision.

In my experience working with insurance organizations, this is a perfect example of a noble cause—helping restore lives and businesses—left buried in a field of legalese, jargon, and insider language. The result? Too many carrier and broker corporate cafeterias sport "Our Vision" posters that erroneously list mission statements (and they're poorly worded mission statements to boot).

This is a huge missed opportunity. The mission is simply what you do as an organization. What's your function? You sell insurance, and you provide peace of mind.

Your vision? That's entirely different. You must articulate a higher purpose for your organization. Yes, you need profits. But if you're successful at your mission of creating or selling what you do, what will make the world a better place and foster a better state of affairs for your stakeholders, including business partners, employees, and consumers?

Your vision statement should express the higher purpose or customer experience that you're helping to create. Isn't that why you are really here?

The vision statement can't be self-serving or talk about something that already exists. And think beyond financials and transactions. Your vision should not be "to double sales in three years," although that might be a good business plan. Of course you want to be profitable and earn money for stakeholders. But what matters most to customers? To employees? To business partners? Why should they give a hoot—or their money—if you claim your vision is, for example, "To be the largest seller of small business insurance in the Midwest?"

Tony's Take: Unexpectedly Finding Ford

I was recently walking up Russian Hill in San Francisco, on my way to retrieve the kids from school, when the angle of the sunlight, the temperature of the air, and probably some other aspects of where I was and what I was doing all came together at once, and triggered a vivid memory of my father driving into our driveway in Michigan nearly half a century ago in our new car—a Ford Ranch Wagon.

That car made me happy, even though in the end it was not a great car: The engine was constantly going out of tune; the body quickly rusted through; the air conditioning ceased working after a couple of Midwestern summers. My father probably regretted buying such a piece of junk.

My older sister eventually totaled it (she luckily survived unscathed), but prior to its destruction at the hands of a teenage driver, I remember my brother and I riding in the "way back" when we would take our annual, long road trip to visit relatives in Pennsylvania.

Yet here I was, a world away from that time, and a flood of memories, good and bad, triggered a single visual: An oval with "Ford" written in script. I then thought to myself: "I kind of like that new Ford Flex . . ."

What are the chances of that happening? Hard to say exactly, but safe to assume they are greater because Ford is always out there, working to improve their products, trying new designs, even going so far as sponsoring bicycles – *bicycles!* – to reposition themselves as a "mobility company" instead of simply another car company. In short, they didn't get "lucky" by being a shrinking violet of a brand. Quite the opposite.

That's the Power of Seven.

THE POWER OF SIX

Don't be evil.

"It takes 20 years to build a reputation and five minutes to ruin it. If you think about that, you'll do things differently."
—**Warren Buffett**, CEO of Berkshire Hathaway

You probably know that 666 is the sign of the devil, and yes, that devil is always lurking in the details.

Brands have to pay very close attention to those details that could mean the difference between doing good or doing evil in the eyes of the consumer. "Don't Be Evil" was, of course, the original mantra from the Google Code of Conduct. When Google the company became Alphabet the company, that mantra changed to "Do the Right Thing," which was supposed to change the focus to actually doing positive things as opposed to merely getting by without being really bad. (Codes are always stronger when "do" is emphasized over "don't.") But it's instructive for brands to understand the bad that will be visited on them if they concoct evil plans to make more money from their customers. This is the Power of Six.

In 2011, the movies-by-mail company Netflix introduced a complicated new offer that bifurcated existing service into separate traditional DVD-by-mail and downloadable plans, and then proceeded to announce a price hike, to boot. Not the nicest thing to do to your customers in the midst of the worst recession since the great depression, as people in such stressful times typically find solace in escapist activities like watching movies, eating sweets, and drinking booze. In response to the brand's breach of protocol, in the weeks that followed the pricing announcement, 800,000 formerly loyal fans showed the company what the Power of Six means by deep-sixing their subscriptions.

Netflix execs were not necessarily wrong in their accounting or their business acumen. Certainly they looked at all the pricing models and determined there might be some attrition, but in the end believed they had a strong business case.

What Netflix's leaders clearly didn't consider was that their move would hurt people's feelings so deeply they would take off the ring, throw it in Netflix's face, and storm out the door. So while the company wasn't trying to be evil, per se, they never really stopped to weigh the emotional consequences of their actions on the relationship their customers had with the brand. Ignore the Power of Six at your own peril.

It took an embarrassing public back-down from that policy, followed by several years in the brand wilderness, but Netflix reinvented itself and eventually came back with a newfound respect for the needs of its customers. Now it's setting benchmarks as one of the leading entertainment brands in the world. Kudos to its leaders for mending their evil ways.

In August 2017, luxury resort Mar-a-Lago got a massive taste of the bitter Power of Six after its owner, then-U.S. president Donald J. Trump, managed to find moral equivalence between the violent and, in fact, deadly actions of neo-Nazis, the KKK, and other alt-right thugs (he called them "some very fine people") and the citizens who had come to protest the hate and intolerance these groups represented. The fallout was swift and severe. Scores of high-profile charities that usually had booked the venue for fundraisers abruptly canceled the events rather than be associated with the Power of Six.

Facebook, largely untouchable through its rise, also faced a day of reckoning when it ultimately came to the conclusion that it was complicit in the Russian hacking of the U.S. presidential election of 2016 by having allowed Kremlin-directed bots to purchase more than $100,000 worth of advertising targeted specifically at people who were susceptible to sociopolitical manipulation. As of this writing, it's unclear what the fallout for the brand will be. However, Facebook CEO Mark Zuckerberg was personally contacted and warned by then-President Barack Obama that trouble was afoot, and Zuckerberg chose to disbelieve it at the time. The Power of Six can have unexpected and ugly consequences.

Twitter, a brand that possesses so many of the "Good Powers," and that bills itself as the ultimate tool for the expression of free speech, went over to the dark side of the Power of Six when it announced in late 2011 that it would work with governments to censor tweets they found objectionable, if the laws of that country legally compelled them to do so. The global outrage by free speech advocates was swift.

"Is it safe to say that Twitter is selling us out?" asked Egyptian activist Mahmoud Salem in an article by Jessica Guynn in the *Los Angeles Times* on January 27, 2012. This kind of breach of trust is a significant challenge for any brand, and it requires extraordinary measures to rebuild that trust.

An example of how it can be done successfully can be found in the Tylenol poisonings of the 1980s, or the Odwalla juice contaminations of the '90s, where the products were recalled immediately and new safety regulations were put in place, despite their added cost. The major difference between Twitter and those brands is that those were physical products, so the remediation was something that could actually be seen by the customer. With Twitter, the problem is more philosophical, and so meeting the challenge of rebuilding trust will be much more difficult. Still, the company has taken measures to blunt the effects of the policy by posting any government requests for censorship on ChillingEffects.org, a free speech website, and by making censored tweets viewable in countries other than the one that requested the censorship.

When Good Brands Act Badly

"You should resign. You should give back the money you took while this scam was going on and you should be criminally investigated . . ."
Ouch. Imagine if that was a public official leveling such a charge at you, the CEO of a heretofore well-respected financial services institution. Think of the damage done, not only to your personal reputation, but to the brand value of your company and the morale of your people. Yet this is exactly what John Stumpf, CEO of venerable Wells Fargo bank, had to endure at the hands of Senator Elizabeth

Warren in September 2016. This Senate hearing came on the heels of a scandal in which bank employees, under reportedly intense pressure to cross-sell products to make their numbers, fraudulently opened new accounts for customers without their permission.

To make matters worse, Stumpf appeared to blame the proverbial "few bad apples" for the trouble, although it appears as though the number of apples fired as a result was somewhere north of 5,000. None of them, oddly, were executives. Senator Jeff Merkley of Oregon called Stumpf out, saying "You say you 'accept responsibility,' and it was the fault of those 5,000 people.'" He then charged, "That's not accepting responsibility . . . you are scapegoating the people at the very bottom." Even the normally reserved Comptroller of the Currency, Thomas Curry, felt compelled to weigh in, saying "These practices . . . undermine the fundamental trust that goes to the heart of the bank-customer relationship."

Lest you think the senators and comptroller were being unkind, take a look at the values that Wells Fargo proclaimed on their website, as of September 21, 2016, prefaced with this stern statement:

"All team members should know our values so well that if our policy manuals didn't exist, we would still make decisions based on our common understanding of our culture and what we stand for. Corporate America is littered with the debris of companies that crafted lofty values on paper but, when put to the test, failed to live by them."

Immediately following that public scolding is the list of values that the company ironically seems to have failed to live by:

- *People as a competitive advantage*
- *Ethics*
- *What's right for customers*
- *Diversity and inclusion*
- *Leadership*

What we don't know for sure is whether those proclaimed values were there before the scandal broke, or after the team of horses left the barn. Either way, they certainly ring hollow now.

Not surprisingly, the stock market also took notice of the scandal's pervasiveness, and began meting out its own form of justice. Of course, corporate scandals are nothing new, but while brands in other industries generally seem to be able to overcome them in time, financial services brands that step in it have a hard time shaking it off. Consider HSBC, which, in addition to the financial crisis of 2008, followed up that bad event with revelations in 2015 that it had been trading in blood diamonds and helping dictators launder money. The stock price has yet to significantly recover.

Certainly, some of the continued weakness in a compromised financial service brand's stock price can be attributed to quantifiable business factors. But just as certainly, we believe a fair amount can be attributed to the more subjective loss of trust among investors, customers, and workforce that Comptroller Curry referenced. In short, the Wells Fargo brand may have been irredeemably damaged because the culture was focused more on the bottom line than on core values or the brand promise. One can imagine that at Wells Fargo, and all the other institutions that have squandered staggering amounts of brand value in addition to more tangible depositor dollars, there are posters on the wall proscribing the brands' missions, and the CEOs likely open and close their speeches with a proclamation of how their brands' core values of honesty, integrity, and caring for the little guy are their guiding lights.

So what happened? Why wasn't the mission upheld, or the core values adhered to?

According to an article in *The New York Times*, "The biggest problem, the former employees say, has been Wells Fargo's aggressive sales culture, which was nurtured and honed over decades at the bank's highest levels." Writing for the DealBook column in the paper, William D. Cohan noted the irony of the Wells scandal: "Before this behavior was widely publicized earlier this month, Wells Fargo, based in San Francisco, was one of the most respected financial institutions in the country, viewed as a kindly, exceedingly well-run neighborhood-oriented bank with only modest aspirations for the rough-and-tumble world of Wall Street investment banking." He also noted that the financial gains from the scandal were so minimal as to be completely irrelevant to the company's bottom line, and came to this conclusion: "The best thing you [Stumpf] can do for your company, your shareholders, and your country is to resign. You have presided over a poisonous culture where, incredibly, *5,300* employees thought it was perfectly fine to cheat their own customers to get themselves a bigger bonus."

If you recall, what is now Wells Fargo is the result of the acquisition of the brand by the then-larger Norwest Venture Partners. Note we said acquisition *of the brand,* because we have it on direct authority from people involved with the transaction that a large part of what Norwest was after was not necessarily the deposits or the operations of Wells Fargo & Company, but the optimistic, determined pioneer spirit that it possessed. There was no way Norwest was going to make a successful play at becoming a national brand with its regional name and reticent persona. They weren't drooling over the bricks, the mortar, or the online portal—they wanted *The Stagecoach*. In the end they got it, and drove it off a cliff.

From our point of view, this was a case where a strongly acquisitive, aggressive corporate culture overtook the old Wells Fargo brand and culture, a legacy brand so powerfully upstanding it attracted the likes of mega-value-investor Warren E. Buffett's Berkshire Hathaway and the eternal do-gooder Vanguard Group, both of which purchased significant stakes in the brand. How much of that value has now been lost, permanently, in damage to the brand? What could have been done to avert this destruction?

Core values, when they are realistic and true, and where there is distinct clarity and alignment of the culture behind those core values, act as a binary for employee decision-making. If an employee can ask "Is what I'm about to do in line with our core values?" and "Would others in the company support my decision?" then that employee can make autonomous decisions that benefit the customer and, ultimately, the brand. If there is low awareness, understanding, appreciation, and acceptance of the primacy of a brand's core values, or if the culture as a whole tends to treat them as throwaway slogans, then it doesn't matter if the CEO invokes those core values in the annual letter to shareholders. Because if this is the case, the culture will not be able to uphold those values, will not be able to make decisions using those values, and will not be able to confer any of the benefits of those values to shareholders or customers. So the brand ultimately could fail, and suffer a loss of brand value, as it has in the case of Wells Fargo.

This means that an organization's leadership needs to author and then fully commit to a concise brand strategy that includes realistic and true core values. Employees have to be hired and fired according to those values or, in the case of leadership, be willing to sincerely apologize, and in some cases resign when it's clear they've failed to uphold them.

What's more, and what's usually missing from these conversations and the programs that come out of them, is that clarity and alignment of the workforce behind the brand strategy have to be continuously measured by a neutral third party who promises complete confidentiality and anonymity to the respondents. This is especially true for the mission, vision, essence, and yes, core values expressed in that strategy. And no, your annual employee survey and management-worker "one-on-ones" are not going to tell you what you need to understand here—there is a very low level of trust that being critical in such situations won't lead to some sort of reprisal.

Finally, leadership must institute a program of continual conversation, education, and involvement of that brand strategy and the culture that works every day to support it.

Do this for your organization, and it will go a long way toward keeping the stagecoach that is *your* brand from veering off the trail and into the abyss.

John Stumpf, it has to be noted, was soon forced to resign under pressure from the Wells Fargo Board of Directors.

Core Values Define Good Behavior

Avoiding the Power of Six is relatively straightforward, if not always easy: Make sure, like Google, that your brand's core values guide leadership and employees to make moral decisions, not just financial ones.

We found that a good way to help ensure that our clients operate from a moral standpoint is to have them write out their core values in such a way that they are action items. In other words, instead of simply listing "Honesty" as a core value devoid of context, turn it into an instructive statement such as "Resolve challenging decisions with honesty and clarity." Now everyone knows exactly what they're supposed to do.

You'd think this would be easy, right? If you know the car's gas tank is going to explode in a collision, that your cartoon character is being used to sell cigarettes to children, that your sales team is preying on old folks using deceptive tactics . . . it should be clear your brand is dancing with the devil. But never underestimate the power of greed, which is part and parcel of the Power of Six.

But if you've got a strong, positive brand that is a force for good, not only do you stand a good chance at making plenty of money, you'll sleep better as well.

Vision Is Critical, Too

Another way to help your brand steer clear of the Power of Six is to have a proper brand vision. If a mission is the "what" we're doing and core values are the "how" we're going to do it, then brand visions provide the "why" we do what we do. This is critical, because as Simon Sinek noted in his famous TED Talk, "Start with Why," people don't buy *what* you do, they buy *why you do it*.

A good brand vision should describe a better state of affairs that your company is helping to bring about. It should be lofty, but still attainable. For example, Microsoft had the brand vision of bringing the power of computing to the world through its vision of "a PC on every desk and in every home." While that may have seemed a bit far-fetched when it was penned, not only has that vision come to pass, we now have personal computers that we carry around in our pockets—and our lives have been immeasurably enriched as a result.

However, as noted earlier in this book, the typical CEO's idea of what constitutes a "brand vision" is misguided. Usually, they either mistake mission for vision, which is a benign mistake, or they replace the brand vision with a corporate financial objective, which opens the door to Hades and lets the ill wind of the Power of Six blow through the house. Get it straight, or suffer the consequences.

Once we were working with a client on brand strategy, and the development of the brand vision was proving to be a challenge. Despite having achieved a fair amount of success, the company had never gone through this kind of exercise before. As candidate after candidate was written, discussed, and discarded as unworkable, the founder and CEO, a hard-boiled, old-school business type, slammed his fists on the conference table and proclaimed: "I'll tell you what our goddamn vision is—we're gonna double revenue in three years!" Everyone in the room went silent. Is this why they came to work each day? To make this guy rich? That wasn't very inspiring. We stepped into the awkward silence with some constructive facilitation, and eventually steered the conversation away from the Power of Six and, ultimately, toward a very positive, optimistic vision for the better world this brand—and these people—would be helping to build as they did their jobs.

Suppose eighteen of your employees tried to commit suicide in one year, and fourteen of them were successful. Would you, as part of the leadership team, maybe get an inkling that the Power of Six had taken hold? Should you maybe have begun to have that realization after the third or fourth?

Foxconn, the manufacturer of Apple's iPhone and other electronics products from trusted brands such as HP, Dell, and Sony, to name just a few, saw such a spate of suicides in 2010 in its overseas factories, prompting a backlash from consumers that translated into stern warnings from its high-profile customers that something had to change. The "no more profits over people" message seems to have been received, as suicides in subsequent years dropped.

If you don't have a vision statement that describes a better state of affairs you're working toward, and a set of core values that authentically describe how your employees behave, how will you determine your true North Star? You need a moral compass around which your valued employees, customers, and other stakeholders can rally. This is an urgent need—not a nice-to-have that you'll get to one day.

The Power of Six can bury you. Don't let your brand find itself six feet under.

Peter's Take: Write It Down

It all began on a dark and stormy night.

Actually, it was in a dark and dingy office of a corporate building. Here, in 1991, as a budding consultant I discovered an indisputable truth about all that is twisted and seriously wrong with product and service marketing: it's about tactics.

Like a child tinkering with toys, too many corporate leaders are drawn to the next shiny object. A tactic. A project. An expense.

Today's technology exacerbates the issue with tactical thinking. You can spend more money on tactics that just get you nowhere faster. Witness the failure of many digital marketing tools that were supposed to solve all corporate woes.

What organizations truly need is a written, authentic brand and culture strategy that is arrived at via enthusiastic consensus by key stakeholders, and then shared and leveraged by everyone throughout the organization. A well-crafted brand and culture strategy is:

- Research-based
- Consensus-driven
- Authentic
- Written down
- Easy to understand
- Widely shared
- Widely used/practical
- Updated every few years

Makes sense, right?

So why is it that organizations continue to pretend they have a comprehensive strategy? Was it ever written down? Is it hidden in a file cabinet or in a thick binder on the CMO's credenza? Has it seen the light of day?

Often firms have pieces of strategy that live in HR or marketing, but no one comprehensively understands it or believes it truly matters. They'll hang dreadful statements in the cafeteria that read, "Our Vision: To be the largest, most successful provider of car insurance in the state of New Hampshire." Zzzzz, snore, zzzzz. Do those words speak to associates? Nope. Nobody cares to come to work every day to help you achieve that.

Does that prose speak to customers? Absolutely nope. Can you imagine your policyholders just so eager to sit down and stroke a premium check so you can become the largest and most successful provider of car insurance in New Hampshire?

Furthermore, a written strategy mitigates silo issues. No longer can an organization's culture live in the HR department—just as brand shouldn't be owned solely by the marketing department. The CEO and the rest of the top leaders need to create it, share it, and take ownership of the whole shebang. Otherwise, they'll continue to argue about . . . you know . . . who gets the best parking spaces, the location of the company picnic, or font size on the website.

Tactics devoid of strategy? Don't go there.

THE POWER OF FIVE

Make your brand a human brand.

"If people believe they share values with a company, they will stay loyal to the brand."
—**Howard Schultz**, Author, *Pour Your Heart Into It*

Five has been man's numerical symbol throughout history. There are five fingers on a human hand. Five little piggies on a baby's foot. Humans are endowed with five senses. The human Power of Five is seen in the pentagram formed by da Vinci's Vitruvian Man and the Five Pillars of Islam.

The Power of Five is a sense of humanity, and it needs to be central to your brand if you wish to achieve genuine success.

A comfy chair awaits you at your local Starbucks. The barista knows your order, but gently probes your mood to make sure you aren't feeling like today's the day for something different. There is some good people-watching to be had. Pleasant music is playing, and the smell of espresso is in the air. Pick up a copy of *The Wall Street Journal* to read while you enjoy your beverage and a surprisingly sumptuous slice of low-fat pumpkin bread. Whatever you need at that moment, you are taken care of by Starbucks in a very comforting, hands-on way, in the comfort of the "third space" that the brand has created between home and work. That's the Power of Five.

Walk past a Jamba Juice, and your sense of smell will be excited by the energizing scent of citrus wafting out the front door. Peer into the store, and your eyes see a clean, white tableau of subway tiles punctuated by bright, tropical colors. Walk in, and you catch the sound of frozen fruit whirring in the blenders and cheerful servers making conversation with customers. You can't wait to get your hands on one of the myriad of smoothies the menu offers and taste the sweet, ice-cold, fruity richness they promise, because you feel they are much more than a treat—they are a testament to your commitment to good health.

None of this happens by mistake. It's a perfectly choreographed play to appeal to each of your five senses, and in general it works like a charm. We're only human, after all, which is why the Power of Five is one of the most powerful brand multipliers, especially in survival staples such as food, clothing, and shelter. But the Power of Five extends into every category.

Walk into a Tesla dealer, and be impressed by what you *don't* smell—petroleum. Start up one of the floor models and you'll hear an unexpected sound, more Millennium Falcon than Ford Mustang. See how the dashboard has been taken over by a giant iPad. Feel the perfectly formed curves of the interior and sink back into that ergonomically orgasmic seat. This is the Power of Five from a whole new angle.

Speaking of a lack of scent, runaway cleaning product success Febreze was almost a failure. Why? It worked perfectly, eliminating pet odors, cigarette smoke—any noxious scent you can think of instantly faded away with a single spritz. The problem? Since people couldn't smell anything, they didn't feel a sense of "a job well-done" once they were finished with their cleaning chore. So P&G put in a scent that was "immune" to the odor-clearing properties of the product, and that signaled to the user that they had accomplished the task. Turns out "clean" actually smells like something. Go figure.

We were approached one day by the founder of a company called "Swiss Chicken." He had a remarkable new restaurant concept that he was rolling out, literally—a mobile chicken-rotisserie food truck—and things weren't going so well. At that point, the food truck revolution was still wandering around on the fringes of foodie society, competing with the image of the "Roach Coach" catering trucks that served sandwiches with ambiguous best-by dates and even more questionable provenance to construction crews and the guys from the local fly-by-night auto repair shop. As a brand, Swiss Chicken compounded this image problem, since American consumers equated the word "Swiss" with chocolate, cheese, precision timepieces, some very tall mountains, and some very private banks. Chicken was not in the picture. Swiss chicken served from a truck at the side of the road was virtually incomprehensible.

We developed a strategy for appealing to the Power of Five. First, we gave the company a quirky new name, RoliRoti (for "rolling rotisserie"), and an energetically friendly logo. Not only did this resolve the confusing concept of a "Swiss Chicken," but it also opened up new possibilities for the product line extension to things other than not-particularly Swiss chicken. Because the primary selling venue was farmers markets, the window of opportunity started much earlier than the time most people normally begin contemplating roast chicken. Additionally, when the truck would roll up at 8 a.m. and open the rotisserie doors, the pale, uncooked birds spinning on the grill presented a particularly unappetizing site, so there would be very few sales in the first hours. Our recommendation was to cook several racks on the drive from the commissary to the markets (turns out the trucks could cook and travel at the same time!), arriving with beautiful, golden brown product on display. To top things off, we suggested throwing a handful of herbs onto the fire so the scented plume would drift over the crowd.

Now, the first chickens get sold at 8:01 a.m., and RoliRoti's famed porchetta (note: not chicken) sandwiches, having garnered kudos from star chefs such as Alice Waters and Bruce Aidells, have the people lining up hundreds deep in anticipation. That's the Power of Five.

Brands are human constructs, so they naturally reflect their makers. That's also why we tend to gravitate towards brands that meet our deep human needs. We want to surround ourselves with things that make us happy, that satisfy us, that make us feel loved. People who feel the need to be recognized for their monetary achievements adorn themselves with luxury brands such as Gucci, Prada, and Jaguar. People who have a deep human need to be seen as "genuine" or "caring" would more likely wear something more down to earth, like L.L.Bean or J.Crew, and drive a Subaru. Either, neither, or both of the people above could be wealthy.

So many firms are missing the Power of Five on one of their most-important brand touchpoints: the website. Two decades after the Internet became widely available, what do we see at so many corporate sites? Words, not faces; corporate speak and brochure-ware, not human communication; buildings, not people; boring, canned stock art, not photos of real employees, customers, or business partners. Breathe some personality and humanity into your website. Remember, there are living people on the receiving end of all of this. Not bots.

Disney is a brand we Americans loved as children, and if we're not embarrassed to admit it, still feel very much attached to even as we get older. If you ever go to Disneyland or Disney World, you experience firsthand how the brand comes to life in a vivid fashion through rides like Pirates of the Caribbean and Space Mountain, and is personified by Mickey Mouse and Cinderella. Disney is wonder and imagination, two distinctly compelling human characteristics. As such, it also attracts busloads of customers and carries a premium price for admission; the comedian Dave Barry once said, "I took our family to Disney World but the place was so crowded we couldn't get in, so we just stood outside and threw money over the fence."

Defining Your Brand Character

When you're finished fleshing out how you're going to harness the Power of Five for your brand, why not open a bottle of Veuve Clicquot, a champagne house that was founded in 1772 and still seems relevant today. Become intrigued by the woman whose portrait is on the label . . . one Madame Clicquot . . . ah, there's a history here! Look at that pumpkin-orange label and feel the heft of the bottle. Remove the seal, unwrap the gold foil, and begin to ease the cork out in anticipation of the payoff . . . hear the "pop!!!"—watch out for flying corks!—and the fizz of the bubbles. Smell the soft character of those grapes. And taste the bright crispness of the wine.

The celebration ensues . . .So, does your brand evoke all the senses the way a great champagne might? Then you've arrived. High five!

Tony's Take: Smell of Success?

There was recent news on the co-branding front that was somewhat unappetizing.

Ride-hailing service Lyft announced it is partnering with Taco Bell to make it easier for people to stop for a quick snack on the ride home.

Ewww.

Brands are not just logos: They're networks of memories and experiences, and as such are highly influenced by input from the five senses. And if you've ever been forced to sit next to someone on public transit who is eating a Big Mac and fries, you know how disagreeable that experience can be. I'm sure it tastes great to them, though.

Well, now your next Lyft ride could reek of someone else's Beefy Potato-rito Box. There might also be a nice dollop of that crappy packaged taco sauce lurking on the seat, just waiting to make friends with your freshly dry-cleaned white suit. The greasy door handle will make sure you carry the whole experience with you even after the ride is over.

Your five senses are going to be taking this all in, and we don't think it's going to be a net gain for Lyft's brand. Maybe a little Febreze would help clear the air . . . hey, another co-branding opportunity!

THE POWER OF FOUR

Branding begins within your own four walls.

"Customers will never love a company until the employees love it first."

—**Simon Sinek**, Author, *Start with Why*

I n 2008, when Starbucks' leadership determined the brand needed to be re-energized, CEO Howard Schultz didn't spiff up the logo or launch an advertising offensive. He closed the stores for three hours one day so he could speak directly to the thousands of associates about values, culture, and how to improve the customer experience.

What Starbucks and many other successful firms are doing is in fact branding, but not in the traditional sense. They are branding *from the inside out*, building innovative, responsive cultures that consistently attract and retain customers and, at the same time, attract and retain the best talent. But how exactly do they pull off this feat?

Strong cultures actively guide employee actions so they intuitively know what to do to deliver on the brand promise. Employees who are part of a vibrant culture are empowered to make decisions based on the Core Values outlined in the brand strategy, instead of being drubbed into numbness by procedural manuals and canned scripts that they regurgitate to customers with all the excitement of a banana slug eating a toadstool.

Cultures that operate from their Core Values invite innovation and informed risk-taking because they remove the need for individuals to be constantly asking permission (that likely would be routinely denied) or living in fear of the repercussions of stepping out on their own. These strong-cultured companies are, as a result, more effective and efficient—and it shows on the bottom line.

Apple seems to have a knack for hiring and training a diverse team of retail associates so perfect for the job that there is an overwhelming presence of what you'd call a "calm cool" that pervades the customer experience at the Apple Store, despite the manic busyness of the place. Even during holiday crush, we've never seen a Genius Bar employee act snooty, get short or sarcastic, or be overly attentive the way salespeople can be in a department-store shoe section. Oddly, the pay scale for an Apple Store associate is nearly the same as it is for a counter person at McDonald's. Go figure.

One has to believe the Apple Store employees all are channeling their "inner Steve," working in the image of the company's late founder, seeing themselves up on stage, unveiling the "insanely great" products themselves. The delight and wonder of the Apple brand they share with customers is positive and uplifting, and the sales are commensurate.

Type #REIyayday into Twitter or Instagram, and you'll see thousands of photos of outdoor-gear-purveyor REI's workforce enjoying a special extra day of paid time off, something they call a "Yay Day." The only requirement for that day is that they must do something remarkable in the outdoors and then, if possible, let the rest of the world share their experience by posting a photo or writing a short tweet about it.

Not only do the employees love the opportunity to spend time with family and friends in the outdoors, REI's customers love seeing that they are not just shoppers, but part of a worldwide community of like-minded nature and fitness enthusiasts. This isn't just a marketing gimmick: The founders of REI, Lloyd and Mary Anderson, began building this values-based community as a cooperative back in 1938. People recognize authenticity, and reward such brands with loyalty.

Don't Just Wow Customers.
Wow Your Employees, Too.

The idea that a brand is a promise to the customer is a bit simple, but it gets the point across. If the product or service experience doesn't measure up to expectations, there will be a ripple effect from that disappointment, and the brand will be tarnished. Almost every person in a leadership position in companies today gets that.

Similarly, culture is the expectation that there will be a certain elevated level of behavior and interaction in the workplace and that the things we do there have a larger purpose than just making the numbers. It's kind of like what you might have been looking for as you walked onto your college campus for the first time. All the hopes and dreams for your future, and this was the place where it was all to begin. Did it amaze you or disappoint you?

If your experience with college was typical, that means it was amazing. Eyes opened. Horizons broadened. Lots of work, but intensely interesting and engaging. The excitement of graduation, and the start of the next great adventure.

Is that the kind of experience your corporate culture provides to the people who come and work for your company? Do they leave only when they feel they have "graduated" and are ready to go on to something greater? Or are they aching to get out after only a few months, leaving this soul-sucking experience behind for good once they finish that nasty review on Glassdoor?

Branding begins with culture. Branding begins inside your four walls.

That's the Power of Four.

Building a Vibrant Culture at Corporate HQ

Please don't trot out that old "my industry is boring" chestnut, because your culture will only be as boring as you make it. If Funeral Directors Life Insurance of Abilene, Texas, can be showered with accolades for the way its culture engages employees, including offering a sabbatical every seven years, so can your company. Use your imagination! Or, should that faculty somehow fail you, take a look at how tech companies are engaging their people through the community-building manifestations of their core values, such as Adobe's novel approach through which they ". . . tie employees' pro bono projects and nonprofit board service to their professional development plans. So not only does their volunteer work strengthen their communities, but it advances their careers as well." That's a win-win for everyone, and nothing engages people more than knowing their work is helping others. Plus, the experiences they have in doing this community service inform their teams back at the office, bringing concerns about social equity and the environment, among others, into the otherwise mundane discussions about products and services.

And yet, there is something to be said for looking outside your industry for inspiration, perhaps following in the footsteps of cutting-edge arts organizations such as the Burning Man Project to see how they advance their employees' understanding of the brand's mission and values by making the movement's colorful history and ongoing vitality the central theme of their office décor. Weird, wild art pieces hang from the ceilings, crazy posters and beautiful, touching photographs adorn the walls. There's a meeting room decorated to feel like you're sitting in the living area of an RV. A couple of dogs act as muses. People hug freely and cry openly when discussing serious life challenges they face. Their office is open, alive, and buzzing with energy. There's also a distinct sense of mutual respect and caring between the people who work there. When teams work in a "special place" such as this, they are energized by being part of a larger effort to improve our world.

However, there's a big difference between saying you're open to new ideas and approaches, and actually creating an environment where these ideas can see the light of day. Nationwide Insurance, which holds spot number six on *Fortune* magazine's "The 40 Best Companies in Financial Services" list for 2017, engages employees through the creation of a "safe place" where employees are encouraged to take risks and are supported even if they fail to achieve their objectives. As one employee notes, "The uniqueness of this company is how it treats employees. My department is like a family. I appreciate the way constructive feedback is given to me, and I am encouraged to grow as an individual. When mistakes are made, a system is set up to protect the team from making the same mistake again. But, the way feedback is delivered makes me want to be a better associate. There is no yelling, blaming, or anger. There is only encouragement." Is it any wonder Nationwide's employees are so engaged and productive, and, consequently, that their policyholders are so loyal?

When you study other successful companies, it becomes clear that culture is not simply about team building, it's about having a unifying vision that starts at the top, and is brought to life through the team and the environment. It is not enough to come up with an inspirational slogan and paint it on the walls. The most effective, innovative, and progressive companies put their most brilliant minds at work to find original ways to make culture a **tangible reality** within your company.

Want to grow? Expand? Succeed in a competitive market place? You need the best people. In order to attract that talent, you'll need a culture that is not only *compelling* but also *differentiated* from the competition. Once you have your culture, establish practices to bring people together. Our top picks?

1. **Get out of the office, and do something fun.**

Team building isn't about sitting in conference rooms, it's about getting outside of the corporate framework and being humans together. Go to a concert, arrange monthly happy hours, take a hike, do a food tour. Activities that overtly aim to draw in leadership lessons or practical takeaways are less powerful. Spending time together, sharing an experience, or working towards a common goal allows bonding to happen more organically and far more effectively.

2. Try something new, or learn together.

It turns out that happiness and learning are closely tied together. When you try new things together you each become slightly vulnerable, and it's that vulnerability that builds good vibes and brings you closer together. If you're interested in upping the ante, go for something really unusual—sky diving, zip lining, sailing . . . think outside of the box, and outside of the board room, and watch the positive feelings grow!

3. Build teams with intent and purpose.

Team dynamics have a big impact on engagement, so it's important to have diversity across varied dimensions. Constructing your teams purely on the basis of industry experience or level of education means leaving out people with important skills such as crafting alliances, spurring motivation, or even having the ability to make people laugh and enjoy each other's company. A diverse, engaged, and healthy team culture will produce greater innovation and satisfaction than a bunch of jealous geniuses all looking out for Number One.

Remember—there are no wrong answers here. You and your colleagues will likely come up with some real duds amidst the successes, but it's important to keep in mind that a huge part of building vibrant, positive cultures is making it okay to fail, and paramount to trust.

Building a Vibrant Culture in a Distributed Work Environment

Imagine you're on the receiving end of an email from the CEO with the subject line "Agenda for Today's All-Hands Call."

Surprise!

Surprise that it came direct from the CEO—and surprise that the agenda includes only one item, "Our Values."

The CEO opens the call: "Today, we are not going to review quarterly results. We're not talking about net-new premium. We're not talking about our product lines or agency commission schedule.

"We're here to restart the conversation about our six core values. Remember those? Maybe you've seen them hanging up somewhere in the office? Are they making any sense to you? Do we actually believe in them . . . are we following them? What are we doing to live the values we wrote down a decade ago?

"These are the questions we're tackling on this call, and with future discussions."

Whether they are national companies with field offices around the country, or global companies with locations in different countries around the world, executives in the home office seek the holy grail of a consistent culture. While that culture may thrive at the home office, how can leaders be sure that the culture is infused throughout the entire company?

While it won't solve all cultural issues for a distributed workforce, the North Star is a set of core values.

Here are some considerations:

1. This isn't an HR project.

In fact, human resources should not "own" culture, just as marketing shouldn't own brand. Guided by a powerful conviction beginning with the C-suite, *every* employee is a voice here; everyone is an owner of culture and brand. The only "employee manual" that really matters is your list of core values. The result will be more efficiency, more autonomy, more personal achievement. Leadership needs to uphold the values, but needn't micromanage individuals.

2. Write them down.

Your list of five to eight core values literally guides how employees should behave. And if you don't discuss and prepare written core values, and they're not freely shared around the organization, they don't exist at all. In that case, workers will freelance, making up their own culture guideposts as they go. The less connected they are from the mothership, the more freelancing you'll see.

At the same time, core values, like people, are somewhat flexible. Offices around the world may have different tweaks, which is okay. "Communicate honestly" might feel different in Chicago vs. Zurich, but mutual trust can still back it all up.

3. Be authentic and specific.

Core values should describe how workers should behave at *your* company, not some other company. "Create fun and a little weirdness" works well for Las Vegas-based shoe retailer Zappos, but would it work for an organization such as a regional insurance carrier? (Maybe it should!)

If your culture isn't truly open to change, then a value such as "Challenge the status quo" will be an issue because as workers follow that tenet, they'll be free—encouraged, in fact—to raise a hand in a department meeting and ask something such as, "Our customer onboarding process seems stale. We've done it the same way for as long as I can remember. Why don't we rethink the whole shebang?" That sort of corporate conflict will be okay when workers trust each other.

Since values literally guide employee behavior, make them personal. Avoid platitudes and clichés such as "The customer is always right" (which isn't even true). Here are some examples of dynamic, positive core values at various companies:

- Learn, unlearn, relearn.
- Challenge ourselves and each other.
- Love what you do.
- Do more with less.
- Communicate honestly.
- Be fearless and wildly creative.
- Encourage and embrace innovation.
- Be joyful/have fun.

Each of these values would be an excellent conversation-starter in the C-suite, in each region, and in each department. Just as "brand" is what people say about you behind your back, "culture" is how you behave when the boss isn't in the building—which happens often with a distributed workforce.

4. Use supporting tools.

Some team-building events can work across the organization, no matter where people work. For example, if a "department of the month" receives some sort of award, even token, make sure everyone in the department—including home office, regional offices, and remote workers—receive the same thing on the same day.

In a decentralized organization, the lack of physical interaction can make it more challenging to understand how people are feeling about the culture, as you cannot read their body language or experience their emotions. Video conferencing tools can build more personal rapport among remote workers at meetings. Online collaboration tools such as Huddle and Slack keep folks more connected.

5. Make them a priority.

Try an easy test. Ask a few workers in various offices, "What are our core values?" If they can't talk to them consistently, then they're not memorable or clearly differentiated, and thus not useful.

Values should be prominently displayed in public as well as employee-only locations, so go ahead and hang them up. But remember that cafeteria posters alone won't cut it. Each region, each division, each office, each department should ask, "How do we live out these values?" Employees should internalize them and feel empowered by them. Because when you have values-driven decision making, you can say to someone you manage in any office: "You don't need to come to me on every decision; you can make a decision based on our company's core values."

Values can't be presented one time. Employees need to know what they mean as part of their everyday work lives. Continue to communicate through speech and actions in an inspiring and interesting way so workers understand the implications and begin to live them.

6. Ditch the annual review.

Let's face it, annual performance reviews are broken—half of companies already know it and the other half won't admit it. Why wait a year to provide important feedback? Rather, use mobile apps to stay connected with the workforce in the home office and afar. Ask workers questions on a range of topics and get feedback immediately. Earlier this year, CEO Jeff Immelt outlined GE's shift to real-time evaluations for workers around the globe; annual reviews would be abandoned. McKinsey & Company have found that asking employees one question a day (one!) elicits far better feedback and data than the typical annual or quarterly snoozer of a review.

7. Hire right from the get-go.

Sure, that sounds obvious. But armed with a set of core values, the recruiting process suddenly gets more compelling, insightful, and productive. The list of values should be item number-one when the conversation turns, as it necessarily should, to, "Do you want to hear about how we work here?"

8. **It's never going to be perfect.**

Like human beings, cultures are living, breathing, evolving. The health of both shouldn't be taken for granted; both take care and feeding; both are a work in progress.

Thus, while your organization may have cultural differences among regional offices in the U.S.—and surely in multiple countries—the key is to be continuously driving toward an end goal of a healthy and consistent culture, realizing there will be some bumps in the road.

Schedule an upcoming phone call with core values on the agenda. It will be one of the most important calls you can make this year. If you manage core values well, they'll manage the business well, regardless of where your workers fire up the laptops.

That's your North Star. That's the Power of Four.

Peter's Take: No Such Thing as Boring When It Comes to Culture

Think your business is too boring to warrant the effort and expense of a BrandShare campaign and the production of a Brand Essence Video? As I attended the Insurance Marketing Communications Association's 2017 conference, and despite the reputation insurance companies have for being boring and cheap, the very best work shown at the conference fell into the internal branding or culture-building category.

The campaigns were inspiring, emotional, beguiling. They had all the creativity and depth of an external branding campaign, and the high production value clearly showed that this work was considered important enough to the leadership teams of these companies that it had been given a significant budget. The VPs and CMOs who presented the work fell over their own words describing how moving and effective these campaigns—the video work in particular—had been in aligning everyone's values and energies toward the brand. They had experienced the Power of Four.

THE POWER OF THREE

Triangulate between your brand's unique attributes, the competition's Achilles heel, and the deep human needs of your customers to arrive at the perfect positioning.

"It's the first company to build the mental position that has the upper hand, not the first company to make the product."
—**Al Ries**, Co-author, *Positioning: The Battle for Your Mind*

A Chevy will get you from point A to point B the same as a Cadillac, but if you could afford either, which would you choose, and why? If you'd like to be seen as practical, and would feel perfectly comfortable with your social status even on a bicycle, Chevy just made a sale. But throw in your deep human need for recognition of your accomplishments by people who see you about town, and we're headed to the Cadillac dealer.

If you ride a motorcycle, is it a Harley or a BMW? Give us a few minutes of your time for a phone conversation, and we'd bet we can guess correctly. It likely would come down to your need for control and belief in the individual (BMW) vs. your need for attention and interest in being part of a group (Harley).

Look at the proliferation of professional-grade stoves such as Wolf and Viking in people's homes, coinciding with the Food Revolution and its celebrity chefs. These appliances telegraph your allegiance to the movement, even if you never cook at home. Neither of these companies invented the stove, but for a certain segment of the population their names are synonymous with that appliance.

If we ask you to recommend a "safe, reliable, practical" car for a family, Volvo, or perhaps more recently, Subaru would come to mind. Volvo used to own that position outright, but their increasing focus on luxury instead of safety opened up a weak flank on that positioning, and Subaru has taken full advantage, especially in their embrace of a broadened definition of what comprises a family to include LGBT-headed households. The Subaru tagline, "Love. It's What Makes a Subaru, a Subaru" is all over liberal-leaning public broadcasting stations across the country. This is not happenstance ad placement; it is a Power of Three strategy. Remember the Marshall McLuhan maxim: "The medium is the message."

It's this ownership of a word or a concept in the consumer's mind that the Power of Three represents. And it's a formidable power. If we say "online retailer," what brand immediately comes to mind? "Smartphone?" You might come up with two there, but what if we said "the most desirable smartphone?"

It's important to note that Apple didn't invent the smartphone— RIM did, with its revolutionary Blackberry. Yet the iPhone, simply by virtue of its touchscreen interface, came to define and quickly own the category. How? By creating the mental image in the consumer's mind of what a "true" smartphone should be.

Apple did that by positing that a physical keyboard was not nearly as "smart" as a touchscreen, something it drove home in all messaging. By leveraging the Power of Three, Apple was able to engineer the lumping-in of the Blackberry with an older category—the Personal Digital Assistant (PDA), a category in which Apple had been unsuccessful with its own device, the Newton. RIM's Blackberry brand faltered, becoming one of the most spectacular examples of a strategic failure to innovate.

Three Distinct Points

When we harness the Power of Three for a client, we look to triangulate three distinct points in the brand strategy:

1. Highlight the unique features and benefits of the brand or product, something we term "Brand Evidence," that distinguish it in a *rational* fashion from competitors.
2. Capture and qualify the Brand Persona, then clearly communicate that persona in all marketing and messaging, as this is a set of attributes that distinguish it *emotionally* from competitors.
3. Come to a clear understanding of, and then directly appeal to, the deep human needs of a well-defined customer, which is called "Targeting." In the case of a consumer product brand, those deep human needs can be so precise as to be better termed "little peccadilloes."

Expanding on that last note, we're talking about getting down to the little things in life that frustrate or cause some sort of visceral reaction in the customer. Basically, this requires that you understand your customers thoroughly, putting yourself in their shoes and getting inside their heads to really know what makes them tick, makes them reel, makes them swoon, and makes them squeal.

A good example is Charmin's recent campaign, featuring a family of loveable cartoon bears to help ameliorate the "ick factor" inherent in discussions about toilet paper. The positioning was developed along a specific piece of Brand Evidence: Charmin Ultra Strong left less "litter" after use, something that a significant subset of consumers had identified as being particularly off-putting but with which one had to suffer in silence. The friendly, goofy, but distinctly non-human persona of the hapless bear with litter on his hindquarters made it okay to talk about this issue in public, and the combination of all these factors resulted in Charmin having a new-found position as the "cleanest" toilet paper on the market. This was particularly important, as the old position of being "the softest" had been eroded by competitors over the years, and the voices of a specific subset of consumers, which had never been part of the toilet paper conversation, were being heard by the brand, which delivered accordingly.

Presenting a Clear, Attractive Brand Persona

Consider for a moment two sports apparel brands: Nike and Adidas. Think of what position Adidas holds in your mind. It probably goes toward the specific apparel, or perhaps the sports in which the brand is most visible, say tennis, running, or soccer. But all in all, the exact positioning of Adidas isn't particularly clear, apart from it being a venerable sports apparel brand used by different athletes in different sports. Now think of Nike, and what pops into your mind? The Swoosh. Just do it. Fitbit. Serious, determined athletes. Boldly empowered athletes. The Nike Brand Essence is "Authentic Athletic Performance." Seems pretty appropriate, doesn't it?

Upon closer analysis, Nike isn't positioned as a sports apparel company at all—it's a "personal performance optimization" company. In fact, it's the *only* personal performance optimization company. But more than that, it's the personal performance optimization company that's serious, competitive, driven, strong—there's a real personality there that is impossible to overlook because it shines so brightly and so consistently. That's why people pay extra for shirts and socks that carry the Nike swoosh, because they themselves wish to be seen as serious, competitive, driven, and strong—people who have optimized their own personal performance. That's the Power of Three.

Repositioning for Greater Valuation

A good positioning case study comes from a project a few years ago when we were approached by Global Environment Fund, a private equity firm that had a clear understanding of the Power of Three, but was faced with a vexing challenge of how to leverage it.

This firm had acquired two companies, SCT and Bully Dog, that produced aftermarket automotive components for performance auto enthusiasts. These companies were very clearly positioned in the Hot Rod/ NASCAR / Naked Lady Mudflaps end of the brand spectrum. But the PE firm never really had much interest in the deep thrum of flared chrome exhaust pipes or were keen on getting more people to add a nitro boost system to their Dodge Challengers—they were far more interested in some remarkable intellectual property these companies had produced but weren't leveraging to the fullest. They knew that with the proper positioning, this IP could be worth much, much more.

What the acquired companies had developed were minicomputers that plugged into the diagnostic ports of the vehicle, the "black box" under the dash of a car, to which your mechanic normally hooks up a much larger computer to perform tune-ups and bring the vehicle in compliance with emissions standards. These minicomputers were reverse-engineered to give drivers the ability to change the settings on the engine—"Flip the PIDs (parameter IDs)," in this sub-culture's lingo—to get more torque, faster acceleration, or a higher top speed. Emissions and gas mileage be damned.

The idea was to take this technology to Silicon Valley and develop it further with hopes for an eventual sale (at a nice profit) to a player in the emerging "connected car" space. However, the current positioning of the legacy brands was directed squarely at young-to-middle-aged, rural white men, and looked as out of place in the Silicon Valley environment as a Bermuda shorts-clad tourist on the International Space Station.

We agreed on an approach to create an entirely new brand, yet not disavow the connection to the legacy brands, which imparted authenticity to the narrative. So while this new brand would largely have its own mission, vision, values, and brand essence, its heritage would give it a unique positioning that would occupy a specific space in the prospective customer's—and prospective acquirer's—mind.

After taking the key stakeholders of the combined company through our strategic planning process, we had all the components we needed to inform the creative expressions that would establish a strong position in relation to the competitors.

From the strategic framework, we first came up with a name for the company: DERIVE Systems. A distinctly Silicon Valley-facing, tech-signaling identity came next, and underlying it all was a Brand Architecture that allowed the company to keep playing in its original market, move quickly to establish a presence in the fleet market, and get a foot in the door for the consumer market. Performance became DERIVE Power; Fleet became DERIVE Efficiency, and the consumer brand . . . well, that's still under wraps.

When it came to determining the positioning statement, we decided to leverage a proprietary and highly beneficial aspect of this technology that really set it apart. While most of the connected car software out there linked in through the diagnostic ports, they could only read and report on what the vehicle was doing. This software actually could *override the code* that set the tuning of the engine without "cracking," or physically opening up, the vehicle's black box, an action which would void the warranty status of the vehicle, which would be problematic for most vehicle owners and becomes a compounded issue for fleet operators. It also didn't require any physical modifications to the engine or special equipment—just plug it into the ports, and the software does the rest.

The resulting position: "A software company that unlocks the power to customize automotive performance, connecting you to a smarter, more highly optimized vehicle." (A far cry from the less valuable, more cluttered, and wholly generic position of "An aftermarket performance auto parts company" or "Software that tells you what's happening with your vehicle.") This positioning statement is strong, memorable, and unique, and allows the company to stand out in a number of target markets. And when you deconstruct it, you can see how it triangulates this position from the brand's unique strengths, the competition's weakness, and the needs and concerns of the target audience. That's the Power of Three.

Another company we know billed itself as the largest law firm in its area of specialization in the U.S. Yet its advertising buy was fragmented—placing tiny ads in small, regional publications. When we got involved, we identified this media strategy as clearly off-brand. We urged the firm to be in large, national publications with large ads. After all, they considered themselves the largest employment law firm in the U.S.—why not act like it? If you indeed wanted to *be* this big, you needed to be where the other big companies were being seen. A large part of maintaining a strong position is to examine areas such as this where being off-brand can weaken the positioning.

Love Your Enemy

Nothing focuses the mind like being engaged in combat to the death with your mortal enemy. Mac vs. PC. Coke vs. Pepsi. The Allies vs. The Axis Powers. The fact of the matter is, having a mortal enemy for your brand concentrates the mind and clarifies the values of everyone involved. That's the Power of Three.

For five decades, Avis tweaked Hertz, the leader in automobile rentals, with its famous "We're No. 2. We Try Harder" campaign. What Avis, Hertz, National, and all the other car rentals will do, now that the enemies are Uber, Lyft, Getaround, and Zipcar, remains to be seen. Those new entrants are disrupting the traditional rental car model with positioning that clearly pits them against the old boys, from Zipcar's cool vehicles making the typical non-descript rental sedan worthy only of our grandmothers, to electric motorbike outfit Scoot or dockless bicycle-sharing brand Jump—friendly, easy-to-use brands that are pitting the community-minded, eco-conscious city dweller against the faceless, callow, bureaucratic corporations that have ruled the roads with two-ton metal boxes for so long. If they didn't have such tailor-made enemies (who doesn't dread the rental car experience with its damage waivers, inconvenient locations, and gas refill penalties?), these upstart brands wouldn't have so many friends.

An important note: The Power of Three is not necessarily best employed against the largest of your competitors, but rather the nearest. Aim for the one that's eating your lunch, not the one that's dining in the fancy restaurant downtown with a bunch of people who have never heard your name.

Tweaking Your Competitors for Fun and Profit

In the famous Mac vs. PC campaign, "Mac" was portrayed by a handsome young actor. He was the cool-but-slightly-geeky kid: Unflappable, hip, and smart. "PC," on the other hand, was the petulant nerd, a bad haircut dressed in a cheap suit, always trying to make excuses for why his dogmatic approach had failed in a real-life situation. He really represented Microsoft Corporation, Apple's arch-rival in the computer business.

This campaign went on for years, the newest commercial better and funnier than the last, until a startling shift in the balance of power occurred: Apple became the market leader with its premium products, and Microsoft, despite having a larger installed base for its operating system, became viewed as a has-been commodity brand and began to fade both in terms of brand value and stock price. The prophecy of the campaign had become reality.

Consider your primary competitor's strengths and weaknesses. Do the same for secondary competitors, especially those that seem to have momentum building, because they could be upon you in no time. Look for "dark horse" competitors in industries that may seem only tangentially related to yours. That's something Sony failed to do, only to see its flagship Walkman product outflanked by the iPod and then the iPhone; something Motorola failed to do, and was forced to watch as the iPhone destroyed the flip phone; something camera maker Olympus failed to do . . . and so on.

A study by researchers Diana Ingenhoff and Tanja Fuhrer at the University of Fribourg, Switzerland, noted that "competence" was the position most often staked out by business leaders when presenting their brand to customers. However, consumer research has found that such rational points are very poor influencers in decision-making, so such positioning, in addition to being typical and generic, is also largely ineffective. Emotions turn out to be the most influential aspect of decision-making. Writing about the neuroscience of decision-making in *Wired* magazine, Christian Jarrett noted some interesting research in this regard:

Feelings provide the basis for human reason—brain-damaged patients left devoid of emotion struggle to make the most elementary decisions.

That's why we always advocate including a healthy dose of Brand Persona and Targeting of the deep human needs of your customers in any positioning statement. Even in business-to-business branding, emotion and feelings play an outsize role. We often hear the insistence in the B2B world that "our customers make decisions on the specs and the price—period." Our experience, in addition to all the research we've seen, however, says that isn't exactly true. Show a computer engineer two pieces of spec-identical switching equipment, but tell him that one comes from the low-price leader and the other from the most innovative company in the space, and you'll see how positioning affects decision-making.

We're not saying this engineer wouldn't choose the low-price option, just that emotional drivers will have an outsize role in that decision. There's bound to be something about his life experience that leads him to his ultimate choice, and if you can intuit the shared experiences of a large segment of prospective customers, you can position appropriately using emotional triggers. That's the Power of Three.

Positioning for Increased Market Share

Premium chocolatier brands Ghirardelli and Lindt couldn't be more different. Lindt is the epitome of Swiss perfection: graceful, smooth, exquisitely packaged masterpieces of confectionery that come in a restrained range of sophisticated styles. Lindt truffles are famous the world over.

Ghirardelli is the American individualist, unafraid to dabble in colloquial flavors such as mango, peppermint bark, sea salt and caramel, or peanut butter. Its chocolate comes as chips for cookie-making and powders for hot cocoa, two staples of idyllic childhoods in the U.S.A.

The interesting thing about these two brands? They're both owned by the same parent company. The product is made using the same raw materials, the same basic processes, and the same equipment. The only *significant* difference is in the brand positioning, which drives different product lines and appeals to different audiences. And a major part of that differentiation is Brand Persona, as we've noted here.

This allows the parent company, Lindt & Sprüngli, to garner more market share. Not only can these differentiated products occupy more shelf space in more stores, they appeal to different target audiences in different countries in different ways. Tellingly, Lindt & Sprüngli also owns culturally distinct brands in Italy and Austria, while at the same time finding a place for its Swiss-branded products on the very same shelves.

Similarly, Trader Joe's all-American, "affordable gourmet" appeal is also a Power of Three trick of the tail. It's actually owned by German discount-meister Aldi, but most shoppers are unaware and consider the store a home-grown maverick. It takes a keen eye, but closer inspection of a TJs, and the more downscale Aldi stores, reveals similarities in the floor layouts of the stores and the private-label products on the shelves. But you'd never know they were essentially the same store by looking at the clientele—the distinct positioning of each appeals to an entirely different segment.

The Power of Three is all around, but you may only notice it if it's targeted specifically at you (and you've read this book, of course).

Tony's Take: DIY Positioning Statement

A perfectly serviceable positioning statement can be built using the following "fill in the blank" template. A more powerful positioning statement would stem from in-depth development of the content of each "blank" supported by a strong set of clear and effective messaging pillars, but if your brand doesn't even have a basic positioning statement then you can (and should!) make one right now:

"For (<u>target audience</u>) who (<u>statement of need or opportunity</u>), (<u>brand name</u>) is a (<u>product category</u>) that (<u>statement of key benefit/reason to buy</u>). Unlike (<u>primary competitive alternative</u>), (<u>brand name</u>) is/has/does/provides (<u>statement of primary differentiation</u>)."

A positioning statement will help guide such things as product development, marketing and promotions, and sales strategies.

Okay, now go out, plant a flag, and claim that position!

THE POWER OF TWO

It takes two to tango.

"We see our customers as invited guests to a party, and we are the hosts."

—Jeff Bezos

Y ou're in love.

A friend introduced the two of you, and although you weren't quite sure it was a good fit, you were intrigued, and now there's no question whatsoever. You keep seeing each other, sometimes in unusual places like the subway, but these days it's usually in some online venue. You follow each other on social media, and adore all the quips and selfies the two of you post when together. You love the little gifts that show up unexpectedly on your doorstep, always from *you know who*. You tuned into a live stream the other night, and there was the object of your affection, draping themselves all over one of the coolest celebrities, literally clinging to them on stage—how positively affirming for the future of your relationship!

Wait, what?

Of course, we aren't talking about a person. We're talking about a brand.

People have relationships with brands that often go very deep and seem very real. Well-groomed brands can be like Steady Eddie friends who don't go a'changing on you. They are unique and consistent over a long period of time, just like that best friend from fifth grade you see again twenty years later and you pick up where you left off. They can be fun but fleeting, like a brief summer love affair. Either way, understanding relationship dynamics is one of the keys to building a brand in this day and age.

We wear our favorite brands on our sleeves, or we get tattoos on our heads, literally—witness those raving fans of Harley-Davidson. We tell our friends all about our brand's best qualities while glossing over any minor flaws.

We'd be willing to bet that you even take your chosen brand of smartphone with you to bed at night.

Now *that's* commitment.

That's the Power of Two.

Fragmented Media Leads to Personalization

For a large part of the twentieth century the relationship people had with brands was more like a forced marriage than a consensual relationship. There were only three major broadcast networks and a handful of national magazines. Consumers would trust editorial and advertising on the select few evening news programs or in the daily newspaper they received in their driveways.

This made it seem like the big corporate brands were always in the same room as you, whether you liked them and wanted them there or not. Get a group of Boomers together, and they can spend all night singing jingles from the commercials, discussing the characters, and recounting the catchphrases word for word: "Mama mia, that's-a spicy meat-a-ball!!" and ". . . here's the tricky part! The Big Fig New-tonnnnnnn!!!"

A lot of the products we all bought and believed in back then were deeply flawed. But we didn't know any better so we made do with what we were given. "Try it, you'll like it!" was a popular brand slogan of the day. Sure, sometimes there was true love—your first pair of Keds Red Ball Jets—but mostly you hung together for purely pragmatic reasons. Today, we are surrounded by a myriad of super-high-quality product and service brands. And no longer do the big boys control the message. In fact, many microbrands have become incredibly successful, driven by the curious and risk-taking millennial generation. Look at beer or wine. Or flavored tea, or some esoteric water.

Since the advent of cable TV, with its hundreds of specialized channels and, more importantly, the rise of the Internet with its millions of channels, and SoMe with its billions of channels, suddenly the landscape of commerce is filled with legions of eligible brands, each with their own set of "influencers" driving adoption. Young, exciting ones. Older, more reliable ones. Some that you've known for a long time that seem to have had some nip and tuck work done lately. Brands that can make you fit in instantly, or stand out brilliantly. They tell people how smart you are, or how rich. You meet them on Pinterest or Snapchat. A friend recommends a brand on Facebook; you go check them out on Yelp! or Glassdoor.

You google them to find out their political leanings, or if they've been a good corporate citizen and a steward of the environment. You trust the word of complete strangers online and ask them if the brand you're evaluating believes in a diverse workforce because you don't want to show up in public with this brand only to realize the snickering behind your back is as a result of your poor taste in companions.

Writing in the *Harvard Business Review*, Mark Bonchek and Cara France argue that the way we think about brands needs to change. "In the past . . . you had a relationship *with* a brand. But in this social age, brands *are* the relationships." In other words, customer association with a particular brand is more in the moment, more visceral, and more personal than it ever has been before. We get into strangers' cars through Lyft and Uber. We sleep in strangers' houses because the Airbnb brand reassures us that it's not only okay, it means you're part of a cool society that's breaking the traditional rules of commercial hospitality. Consider also how we know about Uber, Lyft, or Airbnb. Did we see an advertisement for them on TV? In *Reader's Digest*? Hear about it on CBS Radio? None of the above—we likely were told about those brands by people we know and trust, who were relating their positive experiences with the brand to us. This is a fundamental shift in the way we discover brands.

Listening vs. Shouting

Essentially, brands now have to listen to the marketplace instead of shouting.

In the old days, when they were unhappy, employees, customers, or business partners wouldn't say anything—what was the point when the corporate world set the rules of the game? They'd just slog home, have dinner, pour a scotch, and turn on *The Honeymooners* for a distraction.

Today, brands can quickly get find themselves in the wilds. Workers are caught on video spitting in fast food. Comments and video go viral.

A CEO says or does something reprehensible. Whereas once that sausage-making was largely kept behind the scenes, now everyone with a cellphone and a Twitter account knows within the hour. If the value of the brand or culture is clearly threatened by this CEO's actions, he will find himself hauled before the board for an explanation, and in many recent high-profile cases (Equifax, Uber, Wells Fargo, SoFi) find himself cleaning out his desk.

Customers inform the brand much more than they used to. Social media is a huge piece of this, naturally. Brands no longer can claim stuff that isn't true, they can't have bad service, and they can't treat employees poorly. The people really can bring down a brand these days using social media. In fact, they can even use this tool to bring down a government, as we saw in the Arab Spring movement.

SoMe is not just an isolated initiative. It must be an integrated function that springs from, and telegraphs, the Brand Persona. It defines how the firm communicates and engages with customers and prospects. The successful firm isn't going to just dabble in SoMe marketing, or even just have a concerted SoMe program—it will itself be a *social business*. These are the Innovators. They'll be fully engaged, year round, in online and social networking activity which they will pair with real-life activities that build communities of support around the touchstone of the brand, as Nike has done with its Nike+ running community.

Nike performs the Power of Two dance.

Innovate or Circle the Drain

The worst form of communication is *no* communication. The second-worst type is unilateral, top-down communication.

The best form is two-way communication—open, honest, transparent dialogue. Strong leaders build a culture of transparency. They don't sweep stuff under the rug; they don't hide things. They request, and can take, criticism. Swallow pride. Ask questions.

How about you? This all will take some practice, but you'll be more ready to compete with confidence.

Smart brands lead, not follow, and they do so with excellent, consistent two-way communications and a laser focus on what their partner is doing.

Are you a good tango partner? Are you on equal footing with your associates and customers? Or are you treating them like a cheap date?

We see brands today leaning one way or another when it comes to the Power of Two: They are either Innovator Brands who harvest the Power of Two, or Quo Brands, whose leaders still believe communication with customers and their workforce is a one-way street, running from the gilded castle on the hill down to the ignorant masses below.

As you might imagine, Quo Brands face some serious challenges but make them worse by putting their heads in the sand. For one, they're sitting on the sidelines of this incredible consumer revolution.

With their enlightened social behavior, Innovator Brands proudly highlight and engage people—employees, customers, business partners, community leaders—in all communications. That's the Power of Two.

Jeff Pulver, co-founder of Vonage, recounted in an interview with Dan Levy on Sparksheet.com how he once decided, on a whim, to tweet "Good morning" to the Air Force. They tweeted him right back: "Good morning." It was a soldier's smart reply. As Jeff said about the exchange, "That's cool." And very human, as each of these parties used the basic human tools—fingers—to communicate through a machine designed and built by a myriad of people in different parts of the world, all communicating with each other to get it right, even if they might not know each other, and might not even share the same political or social points of view. It is rather astonishing, if you stop and think about it for a moment. As Jeff so rightly put it, "That *is* cool." And very much what the Power of Two is all about.

Social media such as Twitter, Facebook, and YouTube has humanized brands as never before. Not just because the "Brand You" can get its message out to the world, but because the two-way communication that allows someone like Jeff to interact in a frictionless way with a monolithic enterprise such as the Armed Forces represents a sea change in the kind of personality that brands now have to support. No longer can the man behind the curtain create the "Great and Powerful Oz" that most brands once were. Social media is like Dorothy pulling back that curtain: If you're not who you say you really are, your brand is going to be exposed as a phony and suffer the consequences. You're nice to consumers; they're nice to you. You set up fake accounts in their name or poison a village water supply somewhere and it is over. Everybody is going to hear about it.

Dell leadership realized they could provide proactive customer service and build their brand at the same time by monitoring Twitter for mentions of "Dell" and reviewing the tweets for customer service issues or complaints. Now, when a Dell product breaks down and its owner tweets, "My Dell laptop just started smoking!" a customer service person is on them in an instant, tweeting in reply "Jeanie from Dell here. Sorry for the problem. Need a loaner laptop while we fix yours?" The surprise insertion of a concerned brand at first mention of a problem with their products changes the tenor of the conversation. What's the customer's next tweet? "Wow! Dell is really on the job! Laptop in the shop getting fixed."

People, the *real* people who are your fans and detractors, now feel ownership of brands and are driving the conversation through social media.

Quo Brands hide their people, and relentlessly dish out double-speak, jargon and acronyms.

Quo Brands may have Twitter accounts, but rarely leverage them because they haven't built followers who could be appreciative advocates in the aftermath of, say, a natural catastrophe. They have Facebook pages, but don't update them because they don't think anyone's looking. Their LinkedIn pages don't provide a reason why a prospective employee should apply for a job. They may post YouTube videos, but nobody seems to view them. Why? There is no brand strategy to guide these initiatives, so they are disconnected satellites instead of a powerful, interconnected network of experiences designed to present a cohesive brand narrative.

Businesses must innovate to survive. Innovator Brands grow steadily, even in down economies. Decisions are made based on strategies that have been developed with the input and consensus of key stakeholders. And those decisions actually have been written down—codified into a document that is shared and understood by everyone in the company. This clarity and alignment behind a codified strategy avoids the desperate scenario seen in many Quo Brands, where the entire company is told to go this way, then that way, careening from one tactical event to another as leadership tries to find something, anything, that will deliver results.

Sales Funnel is Full of Holes

Innovator Brands that speak and listen equally will also understand what's happened to the age-old sales funnel.

If you're in sales and marketing, you may have noticed a change here. Today, the funnel resembles more of a colander—something in which you'd wash lettuce. Yes, some prospects are already on your radar, and they're sitting in the colander waiting to be "sold." However, most others are *outside* the colander, talking with each other and finding out on their own about your brand without your knowledge. Because the colander is full of holes, those prospects can enter or exit in any number of ways from any number of brand experience portals. Those brand experiences could number a dozen before you even know.

Think about this Power of Two. What are you doing as a brand to influence those conversations outside the "colander"? What can you do to encourage referrals from those constituents? How can you tango with more potential partners on the dance floor?

Know Thy Customer

Do you have friends you don't actually know? Even pen pals or sparring partners on Twitter get to know something about each other, and might even call each other "friends" at some point. The fact of the matter is, in order to have a strong relationship, you have to know a lot about someone. Perhaps the only exception is politicians, who seem to be "good friends" and have "a great relationship" with anybody who will get them what they want.

But brands and customers have to have a true relationship or it's just not going to work out. How do you get to know each and every customer? After a certain point, you can't, from a practical point of view. This seems like a Catch 22, but there is a workable solution we use with our clients: create Customer Avatars.

Customer Avatars are detailed descriptions of who your customers are in general, and they're a good starting point for developing your strategy and creative expressions until you have enough data on the individual to personalize their experience. It's very useful to be able to visualize the customer, and empathize with their needs. We often develop several Customer Avatars as needed to paint clear pictures of different target audiences, and always do a male and a female version. These should be largely respectful portraits because, even though it can be cathartic to occasionally poke fun at the stereotypical customer, if it becomes habit, this disrespectful sensibility can seep its way into actual practice and become a corrosive element to the brand and culture.

To arrive at a Customer Avatar, it's helpful to have your front line, customer-facing staff such as sales and customer service involved as they deal with these folks every day. What stories do they hear? Who is the customer, really? What kind of shoes do they wear? The car they drive? Married? First or second marriage? What are their weekends like? What clubs do they belong to? What does their circle of friends look like? What's on their desk? What bugs them? Who do they cross the street to avoid? You can even go through magazines and clip pictures of what they might look like if they were to walk through your front door.

Active fashion brand Lululemon has envisioned female and male Customer Avatars: Ocean and Duke. Just the names alone begin to paint the picture, and it's this visualization that helps everyone from the CEO to the sales associates better relate to the customer by understanding who they are and what makes them tick.

This also allows the company to craft a Brand Persona that appeals to this target audience that these Customer Avatars represent. A persona essentially is a set of personality traits that will find expression in creative such as marketing and advertising, and messaging across social media, public relations, and leadership speaking gigs. Sales associates can even be hired on the basis of how well they telegraph this persona.

Meet Me at the Corner of Core Values and Brand Vision

In the bad old days, there were no Brand Visions, only self-serving corporate visions such as "become the market leader in multi-function, transistorized widgets." There were stated company values, but they tended toward the generic or the insipid ("Honesty is the Best Policy!!!") and weren't really practiced by anyone in the company anyway. Sure made for a nice poster near the bathrooms, if nothing else.

In this new era of connectedness and mobility, however, Brand Vision and Core Values have become vitally important touchstones for both customers and the workforce. No longer can they be vapid or perfunctory or simply for show; if they aren't genuine and adhered to on a day-to-day basis, it will get out into social media where the brand can be punished and a culture can be tarnished, resulting in painful hits to the bottom line.

Conversely, when a company truly operates from an actionable set of Core Values and strives to create the better world they've outlined in their Brand Vision, then customers will want ever-closer association with the brand and talented employees will gravitate to the culture. Both will show extreme loyalty and fervent evangelism.

In a piece for *Entrepreneur*, real-life successful entrepreneur Larry Alton lists five reasons customers become loyal to brands, and they sound an awful lot like the reasons you might be loyal to a friend or a life partner:

1. Surprise: Do something unexpected and delightful, like a little gift or a thank you note. Nobody ever got dumped for bringing flowers.

2. Consistency: Use the same voice and manner, because people take comfort in the familiar. If you suddenly start acting like a different person, your friends will either put some distance between you or have you put away.

3. Relief: There's nothing worse than not knowing. If you can't deliver as promised, don't clam up and hope nobody notices. Let customers know you're sorry and that things are being put to rights.

4. Gratitude: People feel gratitude when they receive outsize value. Find ways to give your customers more than they expected.

5. Belonging: Build a community where customers can take pride in their association with your brand. Loneliness is a crushing feeling, and if your brand and culture can dissipate someone's solitude, you've done them a great service.

Honest engagement in a mutually beneficial relationship between brand and customer: That's the Power of Two.

Tony's Take: The Rise of Super-Premium Soap

The soap category used to be pretty predictable: Ivory, Dove, Irish Spring, or Dial in the bathroom; Palmolive, Dawn, or Joy in the kitchen; Tide, Cheer, Arm & Hammer, or Whisk in the laundry room. They were all pretty much the same in price and performance. Ho-hum. We chose them mostly according to how they were scented (or unscented), which was not very nice in any case.

Then came upstarts such as Method and Mrs. Meyers Clean Day, which smelled a whole lot better, were purported to be better for the environment, and came in nifty, well-designed packaging. This soap was, well, it was cool. These brands had personality. They also cost significantly more than the stalwarts, a price consumers seemed surprisingly happy to pay.

How could this have happened, that the soap giants missed this opportunity? There are always a number of factors, certainly, but in this case the relationship between the big brands and the customer had deteriorated in terms of communications and understanding. People's needs were changing, they were saying so in all sorts of ways on social media, but the big brands were either not listening or were simply tone deaf.

This goes to show that in any category, no matter how workaday it may seem, a strong, unique, well-differentiated brand can command premium pricing if it makes the extra effort to establish a healthy, two-way relationship with the customer.

THE POWER OF ONE

Building a unique brand identity requires a singular focus on a clear, unique brand strategy.

"I am One. And I can see that this is me, and I will be. You'll all see—I'm the One."
—**The Who**, Quadrophenia

Y ou already know the Power of One.

It's just very hard to describe it, and even harder to capture and harness it. But once you recognize all the various attributes and core tenets and customer experiences that make up a brand and do the hard work of synthesizing all of these components into a strategy, and are able to use creative expressions to communicate this complex strategy as a single, readily identifiable thing, then you have achieved the Power of One.

Every day, we are bombarded with stimuli, from the moment our iPhone alarm goes off until we nod off to sleep with our Kindles in our hands. A significant part of that stimulus revolves around brands that are trying to influence our choices. Our mornings, for example, might begin with Starbucks or Peet's while NPR or Fox News plays in the background. After showering with Ivory or Dove and shampooing with Pantene Pro-V (while longing for the days of Prell), we dress in our Levi's or Brooks Brothers, hop into our BMWs or Chevys and munch PowerBars or KIND Bars on the way to work. Once settled into our cubicles, we take a quick peek at NYTimes.com or WSJ.com. What's for lunch, Subway or Chipotle? Don't forget to pick up a bottle of Kendall Jackson or a six pack of Blue Moon at Trader Joe's or Kroger or Safeway or Walmart or Ralphs or D'Agostino or wherever on your way home. Or, skip the national brand products altogether and go for the store brand if you want to save a few pennies. After all, there doesn't really seem to be much difference in quality, does there? Or, does there? Branding is a powerful influencer of perception.

So, why do we choose one brand over another?

Some decisions have their basis in survival, such as finding food and shelter. Others are based in pleasure, such as finding love or having a laugh, or discovering something new to enjoy. But the sheer volume of choices before us that can be used to simply fulfill our basic needs (let alone tickle our fancies) would render such decision-making an impossible task if it weren't for the Power of One. Brands become shortcuts for our brains, and once they are wired in, they are very hard to rip out.

Ask yourself which brand is the "leader" in any given category. Two things will happen. You will form an immediate image in your mind of that brand, and you probably will find that image either pleasurable or disagreeable, depending on whether you wish to associate yourself with that brand.

This image may have a title. It will often be a picture of a logo, but just as often will be accompanied by a whole set of memories: Taglines, jingles, colors, and shapes.

Once a singular brand image has formed in your mind, you'll be hard-pressed to ever dislodge it. There are plenty of car brands, but there can only be one VW. There are plenty of Greek yogurts out there, but there can only be one Chobani. There can only be one Gucci. Only one Pimm's No. 1 Cup. Only one you, and you want specific things that affirm your individuality. That's the Power of One.

What is a Brand?

In order to profit from the Power of One, a company has to have a strong culture and a strong brand. But what exactly is a brand? Here is how we have come to define it:

A brand is a web of experiences stored in a set of memories, where a touch on any single thread excites the collective network, triggering physical and emotional responses to form a distinct mental concept that cannot be ignored.

Take a look at some of the most original, powerful, and unique brands, and see if they have the Power of One:

- **Harley Davidson:**

Whether you love or hate those flashy, noisy machines, you have to admit there's nothing like a Harley. Though other motorcycle companies try and try and try, they always fail and fail and fail. Will fast-growth Indian Motorcycles be the one that finally does it? Maybe, but they've got a real challenge ahead of them.

- **Chanel:**

Class in a bottle. The restrained elegance of its packaging and fragrances is made timeless by the fresh, impossibly romantic branded content the company produces in the form of short films that are devoured by hundreds of thousands on YouTube and Vimeo.

- **Apple:**

"Insanely great" products, as the late Steve Jobs, co-founder and CEO of Apple used to say. Design, technology, and marketing all working together to project the image of a brand that so many people wanted a piece of, the company went from a garage startup to the world's most valuable company in the span of a few decades.

- **Levi's:**

An American classic, this brand hit pay dirt during the California Gold Rush of the nineteenth century, and has personified rugged individualism ever since. This is one of the few fashion items worn without irony by hippies, hipsters, hayseeds, rock stars, and businessmen alike. GAP, Guess, Abercrombie & Fitch, Wrangler, and a whole host of denim dealers nibble at the edges of the Levi's brand, but cannot ever seem to reach the heart. Some of you may remember the Jordache jeans brand, which seemed poised in the late 1970s to topple Levi's from its pedestal. Jordache actually was more fad than brand, and didn't possess nearly as many of the Powers as Levi's, so ended up fading with the excesses of the Disco Era. Jordache still exists today, surprisingly enough, but at $413M revenue vs. Levi's $4.6B in 2016, it's a comparative also-ran.

- **Trader Joe's:**

From the quirky, serendipitous products on the shelves to the radio advertising scripts, this retail store brand just oozes "unique." Essentially, TJ's is saying, "We're your authentic shopping buddies for cool gourmet stuff to impress your friends and family." Talk about differentiating in a difficult, competitive, low-margin category.

The Power of One is an innate sense of recognition, born and bred into us, that allows us to make the choices that help us survive and at the same time affirm our singular identities.

Mindshare and the Power of One

Because we are such visual creatures, brands like these that convey the Power of One form a clear picture, or brand identity, in our minds. The most meaningful experiences we have had in our lives have either been informed by those brands or, when a favorite song from your youth is used in a commercial by a brand you hate, co-opted by the people behind them. All it takes is to hear a sound, see a color, catch a particular scent, or glimpse even a tiny piece of a well-known logo, and the threads of our neural network light up to form this concept, this brand.

Brands Should Lead, Not Follow

In our branding travels over the past two decades, we can't tell you the number of times a corporate marketing professional has come to the agency and asked us to give them a brand that would emulate some top player, either in their industry or even in some completely unrelated field. "Make our website look like Apple's." "We need something like a Nike 'swoosh' above the name." It was as if they thought that by borrowing some visual aspects of a particular brand, perhaps they would gain some of its magic by association. It's a common and unfortunate tendency we all have, wanting to copy success without understanding what built that success in the first place.

There is a problem, however. You cannot borrow the Power of One.

Names are the easiest thing to copy, so it follows that naming is where the most mistakes are made. Recall how the rise of Apple launched a thousand oranges, pomegranates, bananas, and other fruitified brands, in high-tech and beyond. This outsize influence continues to this day, as startups attach themselves to names like Plum District, a Facebook app with local deals for moms; Grapefruit, a software company in the Netherlands that promises "GrapefruIT bouwt slimme software-oplossingen met Microsofttechnologie voor relatie-, project-, dossier- en documentbeheer." Hey, no argument here. And LemonPOS, which is, according to its website, ". . . an open source Point of Sale software targeted for micro, small, and medium businesses. MySQL is employed for data management and storage, and can be used as a single database with many POS terminals on a network." Yes, nothing says open source MySQL POS software like a lemon, wouldn't you agree?

In the banana software department alone, there's Banana Software, Hot Banana, Bad Banana, Blue Banana, Straight Banana, Banana Dance, Bananafish, Banana Glue, Bananatag—and that's just the first two pages of a Google search.

Thinking about naming your new software company after a banana? Think again.

Consider the web browser Firefox, which spawned a whole host of playful critters in the web realm, from MailChimp, Lendmonkey, and SurveyMonkey to Squidoo, TaskRabbit, PandaForm, and Storybird.

This problem of copycat naming is not unique to technology companies, but it does seem particularly endemic in the tech sector.

There are even sites like Dotomator.com and GeneratorLand. com, that will randomly generate a name for you. One name spit out in response to a request for a web design firm was_TenMonkeys Company. The second, BarracudaFire Design. PigTen, Inc. was in the first ten offerings, as was SmashFrog Design. Now, if a software program can randomly generate plausible-sounding names for an entire industry sector, doesn't that indicate a lack of creative thought being applied to the challenge of developing a proprietary brand?

Software generators cannot create the Power of One.

Then there are/were the disciples of Flickr, the list of which reads vaguely like the guest list at a Czech wedding: Tumblr, Yorz, TICKR, Sxip, GrokThis, Gdisk, MTurk, Etsy, Scribd, Frappr . . . companies that seem long on brand concept if only a little short on vowels. The excuse always was that all the URLs based on real names were taken, but not only is that not true (they just keep making more extensions, like .tv, .co, and the clearest branding of all, .xxx), the idea of staking your company's brand value on a word that can't be spelled by the average person is dbs at best. What's more, most users type either a name or keywords when they search, and click through to the most relevant results regardless of the URL extension.

This is not to discourage anyone in their search for a catchy and memorable name. Being the first to brand in a peculiar fashion in a specific industry is not only acceptable, it can be a runaway hit. You don't have to look any further than your local liquor store to see what Yellow Tail Chardonnay and its cartoon kangaroo achieved in the wine world.

Right on the roo's tail, however, came monikers like Smoking Loon, Four Emus, Yellow Bird, Leaping Lizard, Laughing Magpie, Dancing Bull, Little Roo, Chameleon, and Pink Elephant, just to name about .005% of fauna-based labels. Not surprisingly, most of the Johnny-come-latelies end up in the discount bins.

So, everyone remembers the original, and the pretenders eventually fade away. The problem? The magical power of trendiness may have rubbed off onto those brands temporarily, but unless a brand is creating its own original magic—from within—the spell it holds on the consumer is guaranteed to be short-lived.

Names alone do not confer the Power of One.

Avoid the Boring by Default Trap

Then there is the dreadful case of the pendulum swinging too far in the other direction: Boring, worthless pragmatism. It's usually the realm of business service companies with no imagination and a fear of either offending or standing out, and it's hard to tell which. You know these companies, even if you can't remember the name of a single one. IMC Consulting. PKR Partners. BNC Enterprises. HR2, LLC. We just made those up, but they could be the names of real companies, somewhere, given the generic nature of this kind of branding. Of course, any resemblance of my made-up companies to any real companies, living or dead, is purely coincidental. And in this case, thoroughly predictable as well.

Here's either a news flash or a "Duh, guys" comment: Initials aren't necessarily acronyms. They can just be a set of letters, such as BNC. Lawyers Mutual Insurance Co., or LMIC. On the other hand, acronyms are initials that form words: Agents Council for Technology = ACT. This is an organization that is all about advocacy, taking action, acting for the better good.

IMC, BNC, SAIC, etc. are a collection of initials and thus even worse than acronyms.

The plain fact is that names that are a set of initials or an acronym are deadly to most brands, largely because once they become entrenched, they're impossible to dislodge. Like a tumor, they become a liability that grows silently on the underside of the company, sapping it of brand value and depriving the owners and investors of the most favorable exit.

Imagine if LinkedIn had decided to call itself BNCS (Business Network Compilation Systems), if Apple had gone with J&W Computers (if you can't figure that one out, we cannot help you), if leading fashionista Tory Burch had settled for her own initials, which was in her original plan. Or The Country's Best Yogurt had gone with TCBY. Oh, wait—they did. Now, even though TCBY has been around for over a quarter century, how do you think that brand is going to fare against more descriptively-branded newcomers such as Menchie's (fun), Yogurtland (endless choices) and Cold Stone Creamery (quality)? Sure, it was the first, but does TCBY have the Power of One on its side? Read what top executives from Menchie's and TCBY, respectively, had to say about their brands in recent interviews with Franchise Chatter Blog:

> *"I like to say that we at Menchie's 'sell smiles' via frozen yogurt. We offer such a unique environment that when people come by, they don't just get a delicious product, they get a full 360-degree experience. It's a multi-layered formula that provides our customers with friendly service, a fantastic product, a family-friendly environment, and a memorable experience. While our competitors focus solely on the food, we focus on the experience— which, of course, also means having great food and service. But it's really the complete experience that sets us apart."—Amit Kleinberger, CEO of Menchie's*
>
> *"TCBY is one of the original and most recognized brands in the frozen yogurt category. TCBY has been a frozen yogurt innovator since their first shop opened in Little Rock, Arkansas, in 1981. In 2010, TCBY introduced a new self-serve platform and a contemporary look that appeals to customers of all ages."— Rob Streett, Senior VP of Marketing, TCBY*

In the end, I would wager that TCBY, while still a valuable company, will increasingly lose brand value against competitors. A lot has to do with the dull, lifeless core of the brand strategy, or Brand

Essence, which is clearly revealed in that quote from the TCBY executive who seems to have an undertaker or an accountant writing his talking points. A lot also has to do with the acronym, which invites comparison that the product simply cannot live up to—"The Best?" Really?—and also pegs the company as a yogurt purveyor, shackling it to a product line that might fall out of favor. Menchie's, on the other hand, has a brand that is not product-specific, and can roll with the changes and catch the trends.

Finally, initials are very hard to infuse with personality, something Menchie's has in spades and uses to great effect in its retail environment and brand communications.

In short, initialized or acronymic brand names are very hard to monetize.

What about a brand like IBM, you say? Sure, there are venerable, valuable brands such as IBM. But only occasionally do acronymic brands achieve the brand value of an IBM. Brands that possess the Power of One always have significantly greater brand value than brands with a poorly-formed brand image. When you look at how long IBM has been in business, and consider how the company has been confined by its acronym, it's clear that even IBM could have used a better name that would have allowed it to shift brand strategies more easily as times and technology changed. Because in the end, we all know what IBM stands for—International Business Machines—and the picture we have of "machines" is very different than how we might expect our modern business "devices" to look and operate. Still, IBM does possess a significant dose of the Power of One, because for a long time it was a singular, powerful brand, driven by innovative products that had no equal but many pretenders.

Brand Identities: Proprietary is the Goal

Because we are not just "visual," but extremely sophisticated in that regard, the best brands tend to spring from clear, effective strategies set up by seasoned branding experts, and from the visual work of a skilled creative professional developing proprietary designs for the brand identity.

Online logo marketplaces may be a quick, cheap stopgap for startups with no capital. But they are rarely proprietary, hardly insightful, and often not even that clever. If you've got an established or rising brand, using a "logo mill" may save a few thousand dollars, but in exchange you'll likely be forfeiting an exponential amount in lost brand value.

As the design critic Bruce Mau wryly noted in his excellent book, *An Incomplete Manifesto for Growth*, "The problem with software is that everyone has it." So when you've got an overseas design "sweatshop" trying to pump out as many logos per hour as possible, you get software solutions, not design solutions or brand solutions.

Nike introduced its iconic swoosh in the early 1970s. In his interesting memoir, *Shoe Dog*, iconic founder Phil Knight soon thereafter was asked at a trade show, "What's a swoosh?" He replied, "That's the sound of someone going past you."

Swooshes were suddenly everywhere. It didn't matter if you made cupcakes or sold insurance, there was something very "now" about putting a swoosh above your name. But more than the cool factor, it turned out that creating a swoosh logo also was an incredibly easy software solution: Adobe Illustrator, and even CorelDRAW had made creating smoothly-curved boomerang shapes as easy as putting three points on a page and pulling on the "handles" of the Bézier Curve tool so that *voila!*—there was your CEO-pleasing swoosh, produced with a minimum of sweat or thought. Every intern in the country was now able to rebrand the company from their very own cubicle. For free.

But beyond the ease of creation, the swoosh was the perfect cop-out for brands that hadn't taken the time to really codify what they stood for, or what benefit they conferred on the customer. The technology companies and dot-com enterprises that appeared at the turn of the millennium were especially fond of the swoosh, because it seemed to describe the indescribable to an audience that was having a hard time understanding what these companies did in the first place. Although real companies with real products such as Intel were among the early swoosh crowd, most later adopters of the swoosh did not fare as well. All the murky layers of meaningless swooshes could not stop the precipitous fall of the NASDAQ during the carnage of the Dotcom Bust as all the dubious businesses plans behind most of those ventures crashed and burned, the swooshes now just wisps of brand smoke that would blow away on the breezes of time.

In consumer staple products, meanwhile, the swoosh became the smile. Pepsi, Sodexo, Kraft, Amazon, Argos (the biggest retailer in the UK), Walmart, and Seattle's Best Coffee are among the brands that are currently or were at some point in the recent past wearing grins on their logos, for better or worse.

In our book, so to speak, Amazon gets a pass. The smile is also an arrow that illustrates the "Everything from A to Z" brand promise behind Amazon: whatever you want, shipped directly to you. One can see how that might make someone smile. It also makes them think differently. When we were kids, purchases took weeks to get to your door; just a few years ago, consumers thought two to three days was a reasonable amount of time for shipping. Now, Amazon has shifted the paradigm so completely that people expect delivery within one to two days. Instant gratification. Whatever you want, whenever you want it. This is one brand that is literally delivering on its promise.

We haven't searched for the thousands of smiley brands that are surely out there, but we're certain there are indeed thousands of them. Some, like Amazon, will have legitimate strategy and design behind them. For most of the others, making the logo smile will have come from some arbitrary decision to copy what has already been done—because, well, it's already been done, and it worked for Amazon, and we also make people smile, so it'll work for us, right?

Trendy, on-the-cheap logos generally do not confer the Power of One.

Getting to a Concise Strategic Framework (Without Resorting to Murder)

So if the Power of One isn't dependent on a trendy name or logo, how does a brand come to possess this most elusive of the Powers?

The key to unlocking the Power of One is to either engineer (for startups) or powerfully express (for existing companies) a brand that is authentic and proprietary. That originality has to be built upon a strategy that captures and codifies true, legitimate core tenets of the brand (vs. core tenets that are entirely aspirational, but not realistic—essentially made-up, wishful thinking).

In other words, brands attain the Power of One just by being themselves. And since brands aren't cognizant beings, in order for them to "know themselves," the key stakeholders of that brand have to act as "mediums" who divine the spirit of the brand and connect it to the needs of the customer via the Zeitgeist.

If your bullshit meter just went off the scale, that's understandable. But give us a chance to explain.

It certainly is possible for brands to grow organically, over a very long time, without a codified strategy and, if they survive, they become powerful and valuable with distinct corporate cultures that hum along like a well-oiled machine. However, in today's world most businesses don't have the luxury of a long horizon to find their way into the perfect niche. To achieve success and build value in a reasonable amount of time, which is what most investors (and employees) have come to expect, leadership teams need to approach branding from a strategic perspective. They must purposely and rapidly coming to consensus behind the core components of a brand and culture strategy. And then they must execute on that strategy with a high level of commitment.

To arrive at a brand and culture strategy requires a significant amount of work by the key stakeholders of a brand. The CEO or CMO simply cannot sit down at his or her desk, fill in the blanks of a framework, and then hand it down to the rest of the world and expect buy-in from customers and the workforce. In general, we have found that it takes the combined perspectives, insights, and opinions of key stakeholders, speaking with complete candor, to come up with the basic ingredients of a strong brand and a vibrant culture.

It's also folly to rely solely on customers to tell you where the brand should go. As Steve Jobs famously said, "It's not the customer's job to tell you what they want." It's a common refrain in tech-influenced marketing circles that social media has taken ownership of brands and put it in the hands of customers, but what has really happened is that a company's current reputation, which is a subset of brand, has become the football that gets thrown around the field by anyone with an opinion and a Twitter account. The direction the overall brand will take is very much still owned by key stakeholders, whose experience and wisdom helps them see through the hazy chaos of social media chatter and focus on the longer-term goals of achieving the mission and vision of the brand.

A brand has many stakeholders. But who are the key ones? Members of the C-suite, naturally. Business or program leads. Folks responsible for corporate communications, marketing, and HR, for sure. Key stakeholders also can be investors, customers, even key vendors, but in order for their input to be relevant they must have a clear stake in the success of the brand. They do not all have to be true believers—as it is sobering for the leadership of a company to receive unvarnished criticism from all manner of stakeholders—but they do need to stand to benefit if the brand does well.

When we work with our clients, we use an insights discovery system that anonymizes the data. Thus, we do not know the identities of the respondents, and we randomize their answers so we can truly claim ignorance if a CEO were to demand that we tell who wrote any scathing appraisal of company leadership. This has happened to us more than once, by the way, which to us says two things: 1) There is a need for more open, honest, and timely communications between the C-suite and the VPs, directors, and managers who have to execute their strategies; and 2) It's inspiring how passionately those front-line people believe in the brands for which they work, and how much they want to see them succeed, even if it means voicing an opinion which could, were it to be attributed, get that person fired.

Furthermore, it takes an objective, professional facilitator to help capture and distill all the good ideas, research, and opinions from customers, employees, and stakeholders down to the most essential elements. And that facilitator must help bring stakeholders to enthusiastic consensus behind the chosen words, organizing and categorizing those elements so that they find their rightful place in the brand strategy. Anyone whose paycheck relies on pleasing the boss is disqualified, because brands are bigger than just the founder or the CEO, even if those leaders have an outsize influence on the brand. And this means someone occasionally has to let the boss know he or she is more than a little off-base, while making sure all stakeholder voices are heard, no matter how meek; and all ideas, no matter how far-fetched they initially may seem, are at least considered.

This is best achieved through the careful analysis of a combination of external research and internal insights discovery, which are analyzed and subsequently reported to key stakeholders at the opening of a one- or two-day brand strategy workshop. Note: The workshop must be held at an offsite location, or the typical interruptions, hallway chatter, and other merciless disruptions will derail the process and waste everyone's time.

At this workshop, the facilitator leads the stakeholders through a series of exercises to help them—yes, them. Neither the branding consultancy nor the marketing team author the core tenets of the brand. It is the role of the consultancy to facilitate this process, guiding it to a successful conclusion, but in order for key stakeholders to take ownership of the resulting brand and culture strategy, they have to be the ones who have authored it. This authorship + ownership approach ensures authenticity and durability. Why? Others in the company, as well as outside communications agencies and other business partners, are loath to alter a document that has so many leadership fingerprints all over it.

The questions we pose to stakeholders are often subjective and projective. The subjective questions are basically soliciting the informed opinions of the key stakeholders, while projective questions usually involve taking the interviewee out of the moment and into an intellectual situation they didn't expect, and recording their salient responses to questions such as, "If your brand were an animal, what kind of animal would it be?" The associations that stakeholders have with the brand are then revealed without giving the respondent the chance to prevaricate their answers to protect the brand. This lets us know if the brand is a lion or a lamb. Asking the same question but substituting "car" or "superhero" for "animal" gives useful comparison benchmarking as well as status insight. For those of you involved in marketing, this is probably something you consider a Branding 101 kind of exercise, but we still use it in our work, as it's remarkable just how revealing it can be.

In addition to the same subjectives and projectives we ask the external stakeholders, we use a very powerful set of tools to determine the true feelings and highest aspirations these stakeholders hold for the brand. A proprietary list of descriptive words are presented to the person, from which they choose the words they believe most aptly describe the brand as it is, and then how they want the brand to be in the future. We break these words down into three segments: 1) Stop Words (actions or attributes associated with the brand that stakeholders wish the brand would shed), 2) Keep Words (those associated with the brand that are worth retaining), and 3) Want Words (associations the brand does not possess, but that stakeholders wish it did).

We take the responses and build them into a word cloud that graphically displays where the brand is, what it needs to shed in order to grow, and what characteristics it needs to acquire or actions it needs to take in order to achieve success. The more key stakeholders select a certain word, the larger it appears in the cloud. We also find patterns of association in the words, which we represent by groupings.

Building Blocks

The basic components of a brand and culture strategy that need to be in place before a brand can leverage the Power of One are:

- Brand Mission
- Brand Vision
- Core Values
- Brand Position
- Brand Persona
- Brand Target
- Brand Evidence
- Brand Essence
- Brand Narrative

Teaming up for a Brand Strategy

We believe the people best suited to develop a brand strategy are those with insider knowledge of where the organization has been and where they think it needs to go in the future. These include C-suite executives, business unit leaders, HR, and marketing leads—and sometimes board members or even a good customer.

A brand strategy workshop day is incredibly intensive. The key stakeholders are made to work hard in many different ways: communicating difficult concepts and touchy subjects; critiquing and editing the products of breakaway sessions, even if it means sending the CEO's pet tagline to the cutting-room floor; and voting on and subsequently codifying the most resonant ideas into your brand strategy.

But it's also energizing. And fun. We provide intriguing objects and toys to break the ice and foster "play" among the attendees. It's impossible not to smile when you open up a box to find a Slinky. Chickens that shoot across the room like rubber bands are simply irresistible. And those building blocks from kindergarten—who knew?

Those playful, right-brain exercises help extract the creative juices. And in the end, this core group of stakeholders is able to walk away with an actionable document that can help them unlock the Power of One, as well as all the other Powers described in this book. Our clients may have experienced any number of mind-numbing strategy retreats or planning off-sites where the only takeaway is "get excited to work harder." So it's immensely satisfying when they tell us after the workshop that they finally have a workable brand and culture strategy. This is a document that:

- Actually inspires and empowers each employee to live the brand.
- Guides new product development.
- Provides sales with an elevator pitch.
- Outlines how customers and prospects should be treated.
- Gives the marketing department the framework it needs to build a unique brand identify.

On that last point, the brand strategy is especially useful in developing the Power of One. Now, instead of approaching a graphic designer to design a logo from scratch, or a writer to develop a tagline in a void, or an ad agency to produce a campaign without context, the marketing team now has clear guidelines on what will contribute to a distinct, clear brand identity. The team then can communicate these guidelines to creative professionals, and judge the product's success based on "Does it capture and express the brand strategy, or not?"

And because the brand strategy has been specifically developed to position the brand as distinctly different from competitors, the result will almost inevitably be unique.

For example, let's say the brand strategy for a fictional brand has a Brand Essence that is "Sharing Heartfelt Stories," and the Brand Persona contains words such as "Warm, Caring, Mothering, Friendly, Approachable, and Energetic." Thus, would a logo that contains a blue triangle and bold, sans-serif type such as Helvetica be appropriate? What if it were the CEO's cousin who had designed the logo, and the CEO thought it was great? Anyone who has had the pleasure of working from a brand strategy document can tell you how important it is to get it all down, in writing, so that decisions are based in sound strategy vs. whims, trends, or even nepotism.

Get Your Mission On

Often confused with vision, the mission is *what* your organization does. People have two sides of their brains—a rational, left side and an emotional, creative right. Your Brand Mission must appeal to both sides of the brain. What is its rational function, and what is its emotional role? Put those two things together and you have a good mission statement; e.g. "Tandem Technologies provides peace of mind to return-to-work moms with our real-time childcare surveillance tools." Or CarMax: "To provide our customers great quality cars at great prices with exceptional customer service."

Without Vision, You're Lost

Brand Vision is often twisted around with mission statements. That's a lost opportunity because vision is a unique and critical piece of your brand strategy. The Brand Vision is *why* you do what you do. What is your brand's vision for the better world, or better state of affairs for your customers that, by executing on your mission, you're helping to foster? This vision should be driven by your values. It's not self-centered or self-serving. Your vision is not to "double sales in three years," although that could be a good business goal. You must inspire people with this statement. The Parkinson's Foundation says, "We envision a world without Parkinson's." Bold, yes? Especially when one considers the organization will not exist and staff will not get paid if that vision becomes reality. You don't see anything here about being "the world's premier research organization . . . blah blah . . . "

The Inestimable Value of Values

Core Values are *how* people should behave in an organization. Values are where brand and culture intersect in a strategic plan, because well-defined values are lived on the inside and shared on the outside. When a company is values-driven, you don't need thick manuals for everything—people can operate, communicate, and make decisions in relation to the values. The result is more efficiency, more autonomy, more personal achievement. Leadership needs to uphold these values, but needn't micromanage individuals. Values should be action-oriented, and speak to every employee in his or her role. Example:

"Encourage and embrace innovation." At all costs, avoid clichés, such as "The customer is always right" (that's vague . . . and not even true).

Stay on Target

Many, if not most, organizations have multiple audience sets to consider. You must be very specific; if you try to appeal to everyone, you'll appeal to no one. You must understand who your audience is, and then you must articulate their deep human needs. In other words, what really encourages them to use your product or service—is it pride, trust, a sense of belonging or accomplishment, or . . . ? Drilling down will uncover a treasure trove of useful wisdom about what drives your customers and business partners. Once you have the Brand Target clearly in your sites, you're more likely to score a bullseye.

In a Position of Power

Ries and Trout defined positioning as "the place a brand occupies in the mind of its target audience," which pretty much sums it up. We'd only add that it's the place you *consciously work to ensure* your brand occupies. Once your brand stakes out a strong Brand Position, that position has to be constantly strengthened and defended from competitors that will try to dislodge it. Think of it as being King of the Hill.

Capture the Brand Essence

Brand Essence is shorthand for all that you stand for—a mantra for all the components of the brand and culture strategy (see below). It's one, two, or three words perfectly capturing everything about what you do. For Chromium, it's "catalyst," since we spur key stakeholders to consensus on an authentic brand and culture strategy. A brand essence could be "timeless moments," "affordable luxury," or "think smart." It's not necessarily a tagline; in fact, it doesn't even have to see the light of day beyond the walls of the organization. It's simply a quick way to express everything your brand stands for, to be remembered and invoked whenever making important decisions.

What's the Narrative?

Where did your brand come from? What has it accomplished in a big-picture way? What's the authentic story, or narrative, that is so compelling that customers will want to be a part of that narrative? That's how you build trust.

Here's a cool narrative from the back of a bag of Ruffles potato chips, made by Frito Lay: "Back in the day, chips were flat, and that was boring. So we made a chip that zigged and zagged, and we shared it with the world. Backyard BBQs were never the same. Because when you have ridges, the crunches are crunchier, the dipping strength multiplies, and your chips become Ruffles."

Boom.

Not only does our methodology point out the unique but often unexploited resources a brand possesses, it highlights the underlying Brand Narrative and discovers the unique Brand Evidence that can be used to make the case of a brand's superiority to customers. A brand workshop also defines the Brand Persona, the human traits that can be ascribed to a brand and help form its personality.

Brand Narrative can be defined as the inherent strengths that bind a brand together in the form of a classic story line, such as "David and Goliath," or "Fearless Pioneer." Often these strengths spring from the corporate culture, such as an ethos passed on by the founder to "go the extra mile" for the customer. They can also have their roots in more prosaic, but equally important, hard-core business aspects, such as "rapid and robust manufacturing capabilities." Brand Narrative can be based in perception, as long as those perceptions are widely held within a company or an industry. It's a universally appealing story—sometimes whimsical, nostalgic, even astonishing—that weaves the past to the future.

You've heard of Lloyd's of London, which would make sense since it's the world's largest specialty insurance market. But back in 1686, it was just a place for a cuppa joe. Edward Lloyd opened a coffee house on Tower Street in London, and it eventually became the preferred place for ship owners and others to get marine insurance. The financiers would sign for a portion of a ship's journey under the dotted line—and hence the term "underwriter" was born. "Pioneer of an Industry" is a Brand Narrative that no one can take away from Lloyd's.

Apple has a culture that produces beautiful, innovative products by thinking differently about things. Accounting services from one of the Big Four could be characterized as adhering to "the most rigorous standards." Nordstrom can point to its professional sales staff as "devoted to the customer's individual needs." None of these things can be measured, except in an empirical fashion, but we feel their existence. They aren't truths, necessarily, but beliefs that seem to manifest themselves in the brand experience.

The Whole Truth

Brand Evidence, on the other hand, are the points of superiority that can be proven in a court of law. A home and garden store could claim

"Largest inventory of garden tools," while an automaker can point to "Highest ranking in the latest J.D. Power survey" as Brand Evidence. A claim that can be put to the test of plausibility and survive is a powerful driver for any brand, as customers put a great deal of trust in third-party affirmations of a brand's superiority. Because people use logic (in addition to emotion) to make purchasing decisions, it's important to be clear on the points of provable superiority that make your brand a smarter choice than that of a competitor.

Say you're facing a judge in a court of law. She says, "Prove to me that you're better." You would use superlatives, numbers, facts, and incontestable truths to prove your superiority. You can't readily prove something like, "Our people give the best service." But you could say, "Our people are highly trained. More than 60% of our associates have advanced professional certifications." Or: "We're the oldest bank in Kansas." "We have the most expansive disability insurance coverage on the market."

If you can prove it, that's evidence. And if you can't cite any evidence, that's an action item for your business to achieve in the future.

For years, McDonald's trumpeted the ever-growing tally of customers served as a changing feature of its iconic signage. While it's not certain how accurate that count was at any point, what's clear is that they were presenting it as hard evidence, as opposed to opinion. "Lots of People Like Our Food" would not have had the same effect as the seemingly actual number of people who had walked through their doors. Back in the 1970s, you'd see an updated street sign on how many millions of burgers were sold. At this point, "Over a Billion Served" is all they need to present as Brand Evidence that there is a reason consumers can trust them.

Project a Winning Persona

Brand Persona is harder to pin down, because just as we have a hard time accurately describing our own personalities, stakeholders within a brand tend to overlook significant attributes, either positive or negative, that go into the "personality" of that brand.

Brand Persona is the image the organization consciously projects. Some of this persona is generally derived from the tenor set by founders, other traits are developed specifically to appeal to the Target Audience. Persona informs the tone of voice used in marketing, the types of images chosen for display in collateral, the types of persons chosen for customer service roles.

As "The Negotiator," the actor William Shatner personified the frenzied, intense, and deeply emotional Brand Persona of the bargain-hunting travel and accommodations site, Priceline. What lengths would you go to get a real bargain? For The Negotiator it bordered on insanity, even to the point where, in the last commercial featuring Shatner as The Negotiator, he gave his own life so that others could live to save money another day. Just before plunging to his fiery death in a bus crash, he begs customers to "Save Yourself— SOME MONEY!" This frenetic expression of the Brand Persona of Priceline is spot on: Obsessed, daring, resourceful—all in the service of saving a few bucks for the customer.

At Chromium, we use projective exercises to tease out the Brand Persona. Instead of asking a direct question (what is your brand's character?), we ask them to project their brand onto something more subjective, such as, "If Brand X were an animal, what kind of animal would it be?" Though severely left-brained respondents sometimes have trouble with this kind of question, most people will quickly identify a projective for their brand, be it a lion or a lamb, a tortoise or a hare.

We did once work with a Wall Street client where a significant number of the stakeholders balked at the question. "But the firm's not an animal, so how can I tell you what kind of animal it would be?" they asked. So we moved on to beverages (fine wine or diet soda?), with no better effect. Automobiles? That worked. "Ferrari." "BMW 7 Series." "Maserati." "Cadillac." Now we were getting a projected image of the brand's personality (whether that was existing or desired), courtesy of the respondents' associations with real-world objects.

Don't Emulate—Innovate!

We recently worked on a rebrand for a respected corporate food services provider that had hit a rough patch. The founder had recently died, top executives were departing, key accounts were being lost, and morale was at an all-time low. We kept hearing how their closest competitor was killing them, winning all the hot new accounts and getting all the attention of the industry press. "What can we do to be more like them?" was the question we kept hearing.

Perhaps in certain operational and tactical aspects, studying and copying your competition is useful, but from a branding perspective, nothing could be a worse strategy. We used the brand and culture strategy workshop with this client to delve very deeply into what differentiated them from this competitor. That was the easy part. The harder task was to implement such a counterintuitive strategy, to convince leadership that just because one set of tactics worked for this successful competitor, they shouldn't just follow along. Being contrarian is simply not human nature, and business leaders, even very good ones, have just as much trouble as the rest of us in going against the grain.

Specifically, the competition had already masterfully staked out "earthy," "organic," and "fresh, whole ingredients," and had claimed the mantle of French and Italian country cuisine, leaving our client with seemingly little to work with. But the workshop proved otherwise.

Within the Brand Narrative, Brand Evidence, and Brand Persona we discovered everything the brand needed to make a compelling case for its own way of doing things, and were able to build a persuasive argument that this way of doing things was far superior to the competition's approach.

We found that our client prided themselves on their creativity, collaboration, and their founder's experience with health and food safety (he and his wife were medical professionals). Also highlighted by our stakeholder and customer research was the superior quality of their chef-inspired menus and in the merchandising details that comprised the customer experience, which extended beyond beautiful displays of the day's fare to extra benefits, such as in-house farmers markets and ready-to-eat, take-home meals to make the employee's evenings at home less stressful. As a result, our expressions for this client were markedly different from the competitor's rustic depiction of bucolic ingredients in the dirt-stained hands of peasant farmers. Instead, we showed real working people (actual employees of the clients acted as models for the photo shoots) enjoying a gorgeous, healthy meal while working together (collaboration), eating wonderfully prepared dishes (creativity), in real work spaces that sparkled with cleanliness and bright colors.

It was completely different, and it worked. Sure, the competitor had the corner on "fall harvest." But now our client owned "spring bounty" "summer splendor," and "winter cheer." The competitor had a very masculine ethos, so we put forward a more feminine perspective. They had rustic ingredients, but we had beautifully prepared dishes. Them: Southern Europe. Us: California and New American cuisine. Most importantly, they were selling the idea that their corporate food service would save the world, so we made sure the real focus would be hyper-local—nourishing the minds, bodies, and spirits of the client company's workforce which, while it might not save the world, would end up saving that client a whole lot of money in employee turnover, absenteeism, and healthcare costs.

The key was to get them to focus on the customer experience, not the components that go into the product. We helped them envision a world where local, sustainable, and organic were a given—the price of entry—in modern corporate food service, but creating opportunities for collaboration and inspiration was their special calling. We had stolen the competition's thunder and turned it into the rumble of customers hungering for more than just a selfish, food-fetishized existence. Our client began providing that "more" very soon after we turned the strategy into vibrant, compelling creative, and not only did the company recover, it became an attractive and profitable brand that was subsequently acquired—at a premium—by a multinational corporate site services company. That's the Power of One.

Out of Many Comes One

So, the Power of One really only looks like a holistic thing from the outside, but like a beautiful stone you find on the beach, a friend's personality, or a transcendent performance, it is in fact comprised of many complex and varied parts all working in harmony to project a single image.

Keeping all those parts in sync is an ongoing challenge. Not only are there the strategic aspects of the brand to consider and maintain consistently, there are also expression of the brand such as the visual and verbal assets such as logos and taglines that need constant attention. The only way to maintain the Power of One is to understand that a brand only looks singular on the outside when there is constant activity and attention on the inside. In other words, the only way to know whether these things are all working together in harmony is to step outside occasionally and look at things from the market's perspective, and then step back inside and make the needed corrections. At its core, the Power of One is a tremendously complex illusion that presents itself to the viewer as a seemingly simple reality.

It's the single most difficult power to achieve. But when your brand does realize the Power of One, the result will be exponential success.

Tony's Take: Authenticity is Key

At Chromium, we call our proprietary brand strategy framework the BrandArmature. We've even gone to the trouble of getting a registered trademark on the name.

The name "BrandArmature" hearkens back to my art school days, where we learned how, before sculpting the human figure, we would first need to do research (anatomy, art history, physics, etc.), create dozens of drawings, and spend hours observing the best and most expressive aspects of a subject. Not just the outwardly visible features (face, hands, hair, body type), but the core proportions of the anatomy, the posture, and the gestures that made each human unique. We would then build a wire frame, or armature. If we had captured those "unseen" details correctly, one could stand back, look at this stick figure twisted together from wire, and actually be able to claim without irony that the armature truly looked like the subject before us.

It is upon such an armature that a sculptor adds clay to form the outwardly visible features of their subject, and upon which the marketing professional attaches words, pictures, memories, meaning, colors, typography, sounds, scents, and even personality to form the intangible sculpture their customers will come to know as a brand.

Peter's Take: Lost in a Sea of Blue

If you're in any sort of consulting business, you've been there. That eureka moment as you're preparing for a client presentation.

I appealed to an insurance carrier client that to compete for the then-emerging Millennial business owners and families, a refreshed brand identity was required—name, logo, tagline—the whole shebang. Why? Just for fun? Just to justify our fee?

No, because the firm already had commissioned a lot of research and endured subsequent soul searching among the C-suite. Like an employee who you'd consider to be a "high lousy" performer, the current brand identity simply wasn't doing its job. Its time had come and gone.

To build our urgent case for differentiation, I started to put direct competitors' logos on a Keynote slide. Soon I discovered something so obvious and yet so astonishing: All of these carriers had the same color blue in their logos. In fact, a number of them used an identical PMS color. Thus, not only did the names of the companies sound similar, their identities looked the same as well. How could consumers or agency business partners tell the difference? (Did a difference even exist?)

It was the opposite of the Power of One.

Out of sheer curiosity, I continued my search beyond direct competitors. I found more carriers with "insurance blue." I soon ran out of room on the slide.

As it turned out, the "Lost in a Sea of Blue" compilation was the only slide in the deck that mattered. The carrier's executives and board of directors determined a new course of action that invoked the Power of One. It was all about clear, unfettered differentiation from blue.

THE POWERS IN ACTION

Susan Smith's Sweet Success

Some years ago, Susan Smith had what she considered to be a clever idea for a new retail dessert chain. She had worked previously in the fast-food industry and thought she could put her ideas to work for herself. As a joke birthday gift for a friend, she came up with a new recipe for cupcakes. It involved a huge dollop of beautifully styled frosting and a booze-filled center. It was such a hit, her friends pestered her into opening a shop. She called the place BoozieQs. The flagship product being cupcakes laced with bourbon and other spirits—alcoholic beverages that have in recent years returned to favor with the rise of the Millennial generation.

Sales have been decent but growth hasn't been steady or spectacular, although BoozieQs finally turned a modest profit after several years. The company has nine locations in three downtown cities, fairly close to each other.

Yet . . .

. . . Something has been bugging Susan in recent months. She feels like she's been on a treadmill, running from one marketing initiative to another. Suppliers pushing significant price increases, while she's been forced to do sales promotions to maintain volume. And the HR challenges are draining—one of her stores had nearly 100% turnover of staff in less than six-month's time.

Yes, things are awry at BoozieQs. And although she can't quite put a finger specifically on why, Susan feels the troubles are around brand and culture. Someone recommends *The Powers* as a relevant read. *Great, another business book,* she thinks. But soon she feels as if the story is written for her business adventure.

In the Power of Ten she finds that short-term sales aren't as important as a long-term strategy that will build her enterprise into something she can sell in ten or fifteen years—which is her dream.

I want to leave behind a legacy, not a collection of store leases.

In the Power of Nine, Susan looks at her logo, created for free by the husband of a friend, who likes to do "graphics" as a hobby, and it doesn't seem to match the aspirations she has for the company. The packaging for her cupcakes are ordinary—just stock boxes with a sticker; not unique enough. The storefronts feel off-brand—corporate-looking, uninviting, even shabby. The latest location still has a vinyl banner instead of a proper sign, but she's been so busy with operational problems that getting it replaced has been pretty low on her list. Again, not what she recalls this project was all about in the beginning.

Sure, we have some sweet locations, but something isn't right. Do we look frumpy? God, I hate frumpy.

The Power of Eight reminds Susan that BoozieQs' social media marketing is sporadic and lackluster in comparison with the consistent and engaging programs run by her competitors. Customers openly express disappointment that orders for gifts or delivery require a phone call, which often goes to a voicemail that gets ignored, and even then require three or five days after the order is placed for production and delivery. And worse yet, the frosting on her cupcakes looks like everyone else's cupcakes, so they don't really make a strong impression.

Where else are we behind the eight ball?

Susan considers herself somewhat lucky as she reads the Power of Seven. But she has been dwelling on her misfortunes more often lately. She hasn't been having as much fun. What got her energized back in the day were exuberant, positive conversations. It was about possibilities and abundance. Now it seemed about scarcity . . . protecting what little space BoozieQs still owns with a few loyal customers.

I'm working harder, but don't seem to ever catch a break.

She gulped as she read about the danger of evil in the Power of Six. The biggest issue is product quality—it's on the decline. Susan hadn't given it much thought until now. But she recalled how back when she launched, she strongly believed that premium ingredients, while more expensive, made a genuine difference in the taste of the cupcakes. In fact, her customers haven't mentioned good taste lately, and she missed the feedback.

Was no feedback basically the same thing as "It's not really a special experience?"

A big food service rep had talked her into opting for cheaper ingredients and generic spirits to generate a stronger bottom line. The taste, and the brand, is suffering and it worried her.

Susan browsed the BoozieQs website as she read the Power of Five. The site is sterile, and doesn't reflect her personality, she notes. It's all corporate speak.

Cupcakes are just things. We are all about a lifestyle and attitude. We are human beings.

Missing from the website are customer and employee testimonials. Missing are photos and videos of people having a great time with friends while enjoying their BoozieQs. Missing, too, is the fun, quirky, upbeat personality she wants to portray . . . because that's how she authentically feels. She decides that all the BoozieQs brand touchpoints—from signage to packaging to online outposts—need a complete overhaul.

How did this happen? How did we let a freelance web designer own our personality?

In the Power of Four, Susan realizes what went awry with past strategic planning attempts. It was all about tinkering with tactics, settling for expense-thinking over thoughtful investment, and it was a search for silver bullets from outside consultants. She also concludes that she had been hiring people who seemed efficient if not a little dull, rather than recruits who seemed excited about the product and shared Susan's core values and her vision for making people happy.

She convenes her senior team of ten, plus three insiders from an advisory board and two key business partners, and lays out a plan to build a brand and culture strategy covering mission, vision, core values, and other components. She says the team should question everything, including the effectiveness of the leadership. "We are starting with us. We are starting from within our own four walls," she says to the group. "Ultimately, we will decide our brand and culture strategy."

Everything is on the table, folks.

Susan then dives into the Power of Three and attempts to write down something about her cupcakes that distinguish them in a rationale fashion from competitors.

Is it just the name-brand spirits? What else? What about our personality around here? We started with something emotionally powerful . . . Are we still communicating that? What about our customers? What do they care about? Do we even know? Certainly, this can't be just about cupcakes. How can we connect with both the rationale and emotional sides of our brains?

Susan decides it's time to find out more about her customers, and that'll take some research and conversations. But she excited about the project.

The Power of Two chapter suggests that Susan hasn't been a terribly strong dance partner with valued employees and customers. In the old days, there was open, honest, transparent dialogue with her team. Now everyone seems to be on autopilot . . . going through the motions.

We're people, not computers. People talk with each other, and lately we've been only been talking AT each other around here.

Susan has the final moment of clarity with the Power of One: The quality of BoozieQs cupcakes alone won't be enough to distinguish from a crowded playing field of boutique cupcake makers. Her current brand and culture footprint no longer would be adequate. She needed something more. She wanted to build something truly unique, and provide a remarkable, almost transcendent, experience for her customers.

Even if people think I've gone crazy, we've got to do this. We're going to lead, not follow.

Susan finally imagines a strategic focus that will guide her company in the future. And she's excited about it . . . Just like in the old days, when the idea for BoozieQs was hatched.

A few years later . . .

Susan and her team have been working methodically at each of the Powers. Things are going well. The teams who work at the BoozieQs cafés are spirited, funny, a little outrageous. They're always coming up with new product ideas, and finding new ways to make customers happy. And there are a lot of those customers, because people have such a fun time at the shops and happily share their experiences via social media using the #meBoozieQs hashtag. The mail order side of the business is flourishing, as orders from the BoozieQs app get processed immediately in decentralized facilities, and the custom-designed eco-boxes are delivered to customers by a fleet of brand ambassadors who ride decked-out, electric-assist beach cruiser bicycles and dress in crazy costumes. They're the talk of the town.

One day, Susan's executive assistant pokes his head in the door, saying there's a call for her from the executive assistant of someone named "Mr. Schultz." Apparently this guy would like to have a conversation with her about her business.

That would be one Howard Schultz . . .

CONTINUING THE CONVERSATION

Find resources or join our mailing list at
www.thepowersbook.com

You can email us, of course:
pvaartrijk@chromium.group or
twessling@chromium.group

Find us on Twitter: @pvaartrijk,
@twessling, or #thepowers

See us in action: Subscribe to the
Chromium Brand+Culture YouTube Channel

We wish you all the best,

Peter and Tony

ABOUT THE AUTHORS

Tony Wessling and Peter van Aartrijk

Tony Wessling and Peter van Aartrijk are co-founders of Chromium, a brand+culture strategic management consultancy based in San Francisco with an office in Washington, D.C. and client representatives in New York and Los Angeles.

The firm delivers value to regional, national and global middle-market and enterprise clients in various sectors of the economy, including finance, insurance, real estate, technology, consumer packaged goods, and food and beverage.

As frequent contributors to global conversations on brand and corporate culture, Chromium's partners have been featured speakers at major events held by Academy of Art University, Agency Nation, American Fraternal Alliance, Assurex Global, Financial Communications Society of New York, Independent Insurance Agents & Brokers of America, Insurance Marketing Communications Association, Localization World (Seattle and Berlin), National Association of Mutual Insurance Companies, Property/Casualty Super-Regional Insurance Conference, San Francisco Chamber of Commerce, San Francisco State University, Swiss American Chamber of Commerce (in Zürich and San Francisco), and UC Berkeley Sudartja Center for Entrepreneurship.

Their thought leadership has been showcased in feature pieces in *Brand Quarterly*, *Carrier Management*, and *National Underwriter.*

More about Chromium can be found at www.chromium.group or on the Chromium Brand+Culture YouTube Channel. Follow Tony (@twessling) and Peter (@pvaartrijk) on Twitter.

Morgan James
Speakers Group

www.TheMorganJamesSpeakersGroup.com

We connect Morgan James published authors with live and online events and audiences who will benefit from their expertise.